By Still Waters

Meditations from the Bible to
Encourage and Inspire

DAVID PURCHASE

WESTBOW
PRESS®
A DIVISION OF THOMAS NELSON
& ZONDERVAN

This book is a work of non-fiction. Unless otherwise noted, the author and the publisher make no explicit guarantees as to the accuracy of the information contained in this book and in some cases, names of people and places have been altered to protect their privacy.

WestBow Press books may be ordered through booksellers or by contacting:

WestBow Press
A Division of Thomas Nelson & Zondervan
1663 Liberty Drive
Bloomington, IN 47403
www.westbowpress.com
844-714-3454

ISBN: 978-1-6642-7026-8 (sc)
ISBN: 978-1-6642-7023-7 (hc)
ISBN: 978-1-6642-7027-5 (e)

Library of Congress Control Number: 2022911558

Print information available on the last page.

WestBow Press rev. date: 07/15/2022

Contents

Chapter 1	The Caring Savior	1
Chapter 2	Words	6
Chapter 3	The Potter	11
Chapter 4	A Song of Love	15
Chapter 5	Availing Prayer	22
Chapter 6	Honor Him	29
Chapter 7	My Portion	34
Chapter 8	Approval	40
Chapter 9	God Can Meet All Our Needs	45
Chapter 10	Despair and Hope	49
Chapter 11	Attitudes to the Cross	53
Chapter 12	Girdles	58
Chapter 13	Debt	63
Chapter 14	Metamorphosis	67
Chapter 15	Seeds	72
Chapter 16	Choices	75
Chapter 17	Godliness	79
Chapter 18	The Threshing Floor	84
Chapter 19	King George VI	89
Chapter 20	The Lame Man	93
Chapter 21	The Beloved Disciple	98
Chapter 22	A Balm in Gilead	103
Chapter 23	So Great Salvation	107
Chapter 24	Stars	110

Chapter 25 Cheer Up!.. 114
Chapter 26 Dwelling on High.............................. 119
Chapter 27 Suffering and Glory.......................... 125
Chapter 28 Come and See 130
Chapter 29 The Three Bears................................ 135
Chapter 30 Birds in the Bible 142
Chapter 31 Beautiful Feet................................... 148
Chapter 32 Faces 152
Chapter 33 This Man.. 157
Chapter 34 Do Not Fret! 163
Chapter 35 Paul's Prayer for the Ephesians........... 168
Chapter 36 Certainty.. 173
Chapter 37 Bundle of Life................................... 179
Chapter 38 Were You There?............................... 183
Chapter 39 Gathered to the Lord......................... 188
Chapter 40 Wonderful Grace............................... 192
Chapter 41 Come, Let Us Reason......................... 199
Chapter 42 Blindness.. 203
Chapter 43 Remember 208
Chapter 44 Living Water 213
Chapter 45 The Ascension 217
Chapter 46 The Race Set before Us...................... 224
Chapter 47 God's Requirement............................ 229
Chapter 48 Paul's Motivation 234
Chapter 49 What Think Ye of Christ? 239
Chapter 50 The Good Shepherd........................... 243
Chapter 51 To Whom Am I Accountable?.............. 247
Chapter 52 Blind Bartimaeus............................... 254

About the Author 259

The Caring Savior

Reading: Mark 4:35–41

And the same day, when the even was come, he saith unto them, let us pass over unto the other side. And when they had sent away the multitude, they took him even as he was in the ship. And there arose a great storm of wind, and the waves beat into the ship, so that it was now full. And he was in the hinder part of the ship, asleep on a pillow: and they awake him, and say unto him, Master, carest thou not that we perish?

And he arose, and rebuked the wind, and said unto the sea, Peace, be still. And the wind ceased, and there was a great calm. And he said unto them, why are ye so fearful? how is it that ye have no faith? And they feared exceedingly, and said one to another, what manner of man is this, that even the wind and the sea obey him?

We are living in the last days especially when we think of all going on around us with the coronavirus and when people's hearts fail them from fear (Luke 21:26). Displaced people are fleeing their homes with virtually no possessions to escape war, fires, floods, and famine.

Even in England, people have had to abandon their homes not because of fighting and persecution but because of severe weather that has caused major flooding in the north of England and in parts of Wales and in Scotland. The storms have been wild, demolishing flood defenses.

Each hurricane has a name given by the Met Office. There were hurricanes named Eva, Frank, and Gertrude, and they were accompanied by record levels of rain. December 2020 was the wettest December on record in the UK, and some sixteen thousand dwellings were flooded in the northern counties causing much heartache and devastation.

Imagine if you were a fisherman and your trawler was tossed about in waves as high as a ten-story building. You would be terrified of drowning.

The incident from Mark's gospel was about a terrific storm the disciples faced on the Sea of Galilee. Some were experienced fishermen, but they had not experienced such a violent storm. The Bible indicates that it was no ordinary storm but a fierce one.

Let me tell you the story briefly. We can consider some of the lessons the disciples had to learn and relate them to ourselves.

Jesus had spent many hours preaching to the multitudes in parables. When evening was approaching, He got into a boat with His disciples and told them to row to the other side of the lake. Jesus was tired and fell asleep in the stern. Then without warning, a violent storm arose, and the boat began filling with water. His disciples were terrified, believing they would drown. All this time, Jesus was asleep. The disciples woke Him with the cry "Master, don't You care for us? We are going to perish in the sea."

The Bible states that Jesus got up, rebuked the wind, and

said to the sea, "Peace, be still." The wind ceased, and there was a great calm. He asked His disciples, "Why are you afraid? Do you still have no faith?" (Mark 4:40 TLB). The disciples feared exceedingly and asked one another, "Who is this man, that even the winds and seas obey him?" (Mark 4:41 TLB). We know He is the Lord of nature with power over disease, demons, death, sin, and the elements. There are lessons the disciples had to learn, and they are the same lessons for us today. They are based on the three questions in the reading: Who is this man? Master, don't you care? and Where is your faith?

Who Is This Man?

The evidence of the New Testament shows that Jesus was truly human; He experienced hunger and thirst, He wept, and perhaps more poignantly, He felt pain. In this case, He was tired after a long day of preaching and needed to recover His strength. He was, however, different from all other human beings in that He never sinned: "For He [God] hath made him to be sin for us, who knew no sin" (2 Corinthians 5:21). His followers knew what it was to be human and sinful, and their problem was that they did not understand that Jesus could be a sinless human being and be divine at the same time.

In the midst of the storm, they were frantic. Had they forgotten that Jesus had told them to go to the other side of the lake? That was a promise by Jesus that they would get there, and nothing, not even the storm, would defeat His purpose. They had seen other miracles performed by their Master, but in their present situation, they failed to grasp that Jesus was able to control the wind and the waves.

Do you fully appreciate that Jesus is truly man and truly God and that there is no storm in your life He cannot calm?

Master, Don't You Care?

Out of ignorance, the disciples asked Him, "Master, don't You care?" They did not know what we know—how He would be crucified for us because He cared for us. In 1 Peter 5:7 Peter exhorted his readers to cast all their cares upon the Lord: "Casting all your care upon him; for he careth for you."

In this verse, we have humankind's cares and God's cares. Humankind's cares are the cares of this world that Jesus talked about in the parable of the sower (Mark 4:19). The seed of the Word of God falls upon thorny ground, and it chokes it. The thorns are the cares of this world. Jesus also described humankind's cares as "the cares of this life" (Luke 21:34).

As believers, we can have the assurance that God cares for us in all situations.

> God is our refuge and strength, a very present help in trouble. Therefore will not we fear, although the earth be removed, and though the mountains be carried into the midst of the sea; though the waters thereof roar and be troubled, though the mountains shake with the swelling thereof. Selah. (Psalm 46:1–3)

Where Is Your Faith?

The disciples lacked faith and trust and were thus afraid. If we trust in God, we ought not be afraid. Jesus said, "Let not your heart be troubled. You believe in God, believe also in Me" (John 14:1–2 NKJV).

Faith is trusting God alone to do the impossible and save us. Had not Jesus told them to go to the other side of the lake? He had made a promise that He would keep despite the storm. Faith is fundamental for those who would be followers of Christ. It is that for which our Lord seeks.

> Nevertheless, when the Son of man cometh, shall He find faith on the earth? (Luke 18:8)

Faith is equally important for those who would follow Christ today. It is by faith that we are saved from our sins. We are to live by faith.

Faith is the shield that protects us from satanic attack.

> Put on the whole armour of God, that ye may be able to stand against the wiles of the devil. For we wrestle not against flesh and blood, but against principalities, against powers, against the rulers of the darkness of this world, against spiritual wickedness in high places. Wherefore take unto you the whole armour of God, that ye may be able to withstand in the evil day, and having done all, to stand. Stand therefore, having your loins girt about with truth, and having on the breastplate of righteousness. And your feet shod with the preparation of the gospel of peace. Above all, taking the shield of faith, wherewith ye shall be able to quench all the fiery darts of the wicked. And take the helmet of salvation, and the sword of the Spirit, which is the word of God. (Ephesians 6:11–17)

We read in Hebrews 11:6 that without faith, it is impossible to please God.

With Christ in the vessel, we can smile at the storm.

2

Words

Readings: Matthew 8:1–13, Luke 4:22, and Luke 4:32

The Christian preacher, Charles Capps wrote, "Words are among the most important things in the universe." We communicate with them. We convey messages from one person to another. We would be lost without them. We would be dumb.

Just consider how the means of communication have improved over the last two hundred years. Before the telephone was invented, beacons of fire were used to communicate messages to people over a distance; the Native Americans used smoke signals. In my younger days, I taught semaphore to the boys in the Boys' Brigade. Morse code proved invaluable for the armed forces to communicate with each other during the wars.

The *Oxford Dictionary* contains over 300,000 words though it is said that there are 1 million words in English.

The word *nice* meant "stupid" or "foolish" in the thirteenth century, and the word *silly* meant "happy" in the eleventh century. So I suppose you could have said in those days that we were silly but not nice, meaning we were happy but not foolish.

Words can be spoken or written. The Wycliffe Bible Translators estimate that there are around 2,200 language groups without written words.

"Sticks and stones may break my bones, but words can never hurt me." Oh yes they can. Can you remember hurtful words someone spoke to you? What about written and spoken words of humankind? Can they be trusted? Are they reliable? No. The words of humans can be fallible, fickle, unreliable, and dishonest. Think of the tragedy of all those failed marriages caused by broken vows.

The good news of the Christian faith is that God has spoken to this sad world with a word of hope, a word that brings blessing and eternal life to those who trust His Word concerning His Son, the Lord Jesus Christ. His Word is truth; it is reliable.

The world today is floundering in a state of fear because it has ignored God's Word. If left to our own devices, we would end up in hell because we are all sinners. But the good news is that God has communicated with humankind through His Word, the Bible; He inspired its 775,000 words.

God is the author of words. Genesis is the book of beginnings. In chapter 1, verse 3, God said, "Let there be light!"

1. His Word Is a Word of Power

By His word, He created the worlds. "By the word of the Lord were the heavens made" (Psalm 33:6). "He upholds all things by the word of His power" (Hebrews 1:3).

In the beginning of creation, God said, "Let there be light, and there was light. And it was so." And Jesus rebuked the wind and the sea with words, and he told Lazarus, who had been dead four days, "Lazarus, come forth!" and Lazarus came alive again.

Matthew 8 recounts the healing of the centurion's servant, where we learn that the word of Jesus is powerful. The centurion said, "Speak the word only and my servant shall be healed." What great faith! Matthew said that Jesus marveled and said to the people, "I have not found so great faith, no not in Israel." Yes, He is looking for our faith, our trust in Him. Does He marvel as He looks into our lives? Does He find great faith there?

One reason the Lord's word was powerful was that it was spoken with authority. Authority depends on the credentials of the person giving the order. A private cannot give an order to a general. I cannot tell the chancellor of the exchequer when to increase the bank rate. It depends upon authority. The centurion recognized that Jesus had authority to heal a dying man from a distance with just a word; he believed Jesus had power over nature.

One miracle Jesus performed brought out His authority clearly; it is in the next chapter of Matthew, and in more detail in Mark 2; it also took place in Capernaum. We read of the paralyzed man brought to Jesus by his friends for healing. Since there was a crowd in the house where Jesus was, they carried him to the roof and let him down on his stretcher through a hole in the roof. There, he was laid at the feet of Jesus. Before healing his paralyzed body, Jesus dealt with the man's greatest need—the healing of his soul. He said to the man, "Son, thy sins are forgiven thee."

At that, the Jewish religious leaders thought, *That's blasphemy! Does He think He's God?* (Matthew 9:3–4). Jesus knew what they were thinking and told them, "I will prove to you that the Son of Man has the authority on earth to forgive sins." Then Jesus turned to the paralyzed man and said, "Stand up, pick up your mat, and go home!" (Matthew 9:6 NLT).

2. *It Is a Word of Illumination*

"Thy word is a lamp unto my feet and a light unto my path" (Psalm 119:105). It teaches us to walk straight to avoid obstacles in our lives.

3. It Is a Word of Instruction

> All scripture is given by inspiration of God and is profitable for instruction. (2 Timothy 3:16)

> Thy word have I hid in my heart that I might not sin against Thee. (Psalm 119:11)

4. The Word of God Is the Living Word

It is the word of life, the bread of life: "Man shall not live by bread alone but by every word that proceeds from the mouth of God" (Luke 4:4). We need God's Word to sustain our spiritual growth just as we need bread to sustain our physical selves. Remember Peter's response to the Lord Jesus: "Lord to whom shall we go? You have the words of eternal life" (John 6:68). He realized that the words of Jesus were the source of eternal life.

5. The Word of God Is Truth

John 17:17 states, "Thy word is truth [Jesus]." It is true and in accordance with fact and reality. We hear so much these days about fake news. We do not know what to believe sometimes, even from so-called experts and political leaders. But one thing is certain—God's Word is truth.

6. God's Word Is Everlasting

> But the word of the Lord endureth forever. And this is the word which by the gospel is preached unto you. (1 Peter 1:25)

Jesus said His words would not pass away even though the heaven and earth shall pass away.

7. *Jesus Is the Incarnate Word of God*

Hebrews 1 tells us that in these last days, God has spoken to us by His Son. John described Jesus in his gospel as the Word: "In the beginning was the Word, and the Word was with God and the Word was God ... the Word was made flesh and dwelt among us." God had spoken through the prophets, but in the main, His words were ignored. However, in these last days, He has spoken by His Son Jesus Christ.

When Jesus was on earth, the people wondered at His gracious words, not His clever words (Luke 4:22).

Colossians 3:16–17 stresses the importance of knowing God's Word.

> Let the word of Christ dwell in you richly in all wisdom; teaching and admonishing one another in psalms and hymns and spiritual songs, singing with grace in your hearts to the Lord. And whatsoever ye do in word or deed, do all in the name of the Lord Jesus, giving thanks to God and the Father by him.

The Potter

3

But now, O Lord, thou art our father; we are the clay, and thou, our potter; and we all are the work of thy hand. (Isaiah 64:8)

The Name

We lived for thirty years in the Potteries in North Staffordshire, where world-famous ceramics companies were located— Wedgewood, Royal Doulton, Minton, and others. What makes the pottery famous and valuable? The name.

The Bible says Christians are "called by His name."

When Saul was directed to Ananias's house in Damascus, the Lord said to Ananias, "Saul is a chosen vessel unto me, to bear My name before the Gentiles, and kings, and the children of Israel" (Acts 9:15).

In Acts 15:13–18 (TLB), we read that Paul was in Antioch to deal with a division among the believers about circumcision.

> When they had finished, James took the floor. Brothers, he said, listen to me. Peter has told you

about the time God first visited the Gentiles to take from them a people to bring honor to his name.

This fact of Gentile conversion agrees with what the prophets had predicted. For instance, this passage is from the prophet Amos.

Afterwards says the Lord, I will return and renew the broken contract with David, so that Gentiles, too, will find the Lord—all those marked with my name. That is what the Lord says, who reveals his plans made from the beginning. (Acts 15:17 TLB)

What a privilege that we believers are called by His name. It was in Antioch where His followers were first called Christians. Peter referred to the name "Christian" in 1 Peter 4:16: "If any man suffer as a Christian, let him not be ashamed; but let him glorify God on this behalf." The NLT renders this verse as "It is no shame to suffer for being a Christian. Praise God for the privilege of being called by his name!" In the NIV, the verse ends with "Praise God that you bear that Name."

Bearing the name of Christ brings responsibility not to dishonor His name. It also requires boldness. Many Christians have suffered martyrdom for being loyal to Christ. There is a contrast in the action of the apostle Peter who had denied being a follower of Jesus, saying "I know not this man." (Mark 14:71).

The Clay

Ceramics are made from clay. Some would say clay is good only for growing roses. What is clay? A smelly, dirty, slimy substance like mud, like us in the sight of God. But in the hands of the Potter, the clay is transformed into something new.

Though Paul was to bear the name of Christ (what an honor!), he was only clay. But on the road to Damascus, he was changed to a vessel of honor to bear the name of Christ. If you are a true believer, then you too will be changed. The Bible states that if anyone is in Christ, he or she is a new creation, and we honor His name.

Where does the clay come from? The pit! We remember a beloved brother who in his prayer would often say, "Lord, You took me out of the pit, the pit!" That is precisely what the Lord has done for us just as the psalmist explained in Psalm 40:1–2

> I waited patiently for the Lord; and he inclined unto me and heard my cry. He brought me up also out of an horrible pit, out of the miry clay, and set my feet upon a rock, and established my goings.

The Potter

The skilled potter moulds the formless lump of clay on a wheel with his hands and feet on a treadle and fashions it into a beautiful object. When Jesus was resurrected, He appeared to His disciples and showed them His hands and feet.

Jesus is like the Potter who changes a horrible lump of clay into a beautiful object. He did it by being crucified; He suffered at the hands of God and paid the penalty of our sins.

Unfortunately, the unbeliever has said in his heart, just as the prophet Isaiah predicted in Isaiah 29:15–16 (NLT).

> The Lord can't see us, they say. He doesn't know what's going on! How foolish! He is the Potter, and He is certainly greater than you or me, the

clay! Should the created thing say of the one who made it, He did not make me? Does a jar say, The potter who made me is stupid?

Today evolutionism passes as high science denying that we were formed by the Potter. How wonderful to know that the Potter is still working on us and that one day, He will produce a masterpiece that will be fit for His presence in heaven. Paul wrote,

> For our citizenship is in heaven; whence also we wait for a Saviour, the Lord Jesus Christ, Who shall fashion anew the body of our humiliation that it may be conformed to the body of his glory, according to the working whereby he is able even to subject all things unto himself. (Philippians 3:20–21 ASV)

Thank you, Lord.

A Song of Love

4

Reading: Psalm 45

During His conversation with the two disciples on the road to Emmaus, we read in Luke 24:27 that "beginning at Moses and all the prophets Jesus expounded unto them in all the scriptures the things concerning Himself." The first eight verses of this beautiful Psalm 45 give us an instance of what Jesus told those disciples of the things concerning Himself.

> My heart is indicting a good matter: I speak of the things which I have made touching the king: my tongue is the pen of a ready writer. Thou art fairer than the children of men: grace is poured into thy lips: therefore, God hath blessed thee for ever.
>
> Gird thy sword upon thy thigh, O most mighty, with thy glory and thy majesty. And in thy majesty ride prosperously because of truth and meekness and righteousness; and thy right hand shall teach thee terrible [awesome] things. Thine arrows are

sharp in the heart of the king's enemies; whereby the people fall under thee.

Thy throne, O God, is for ever and ever: the sceptre of thy kingdom is a right sceptre. Thou lovest righteousness, and hatest wickedness: therefore God, thy God, hath anointed thee with the oil of gladness above thy fellows. All thy garments smell of myrrh, and aloes, and cassia, out of the ivory palaces, whereby they have made thee glad.

In this psalm, we have a picture of the Lord Jesus being a hymn, a song of love composed for the marriage of a king to a princess. It was possibly Solomon to Pharoah's daughter extolling the beauty and majesty of the king and His bride. The writer must have had a prophetic view of one who is greater than Solomon, for much of what He writes concerns the coming King, the Bridegroom, and His bride, the church.

It is a Messianic psalm as confirmed by Hebrews 1:8–9, where the writer quotes from verses 6 and 7 of the psalm: "Thy throne, O God, is for ever and ever." In verses 2 to 9, the psalmist addresses the king extolling His glories. Let's look at the emotional impulse that caused the psalmist to compose this song.

As I said, it is a song of love. In verse 1, the writer says, "My heart is indicting a good matter." What does it mean? Well, the word *indicting* means "bubbling over" with the warmth of love and affection, not a cold heart, as he has been contemplating the glory of the king. The good matter concerns the king. He does not say his brain, but his heart, the seat of his emotions, is bubbling over. As believers, our cold, stony hearts have been made hearts of flesh. The Holy Spirit dwelling in us has planted the love of God in our hearts so that we can appreciate His beauty and glory.

Before we were saved, our hearts were deceitful above all things and desperately wicked (Jeremiah 17:9), but then the day came when we cried out to the Lord just like King David, "Create in me a clean heart" (Psalm 51:10).

Sometimes, when we come to worship the Lord, we come with a cold heart instead of a warm heart. Are our hearts bubbling over? Are we thrilled with our meditation of the Lord Jesus? This song, being a messianic psalm, speaks of King Jesus. What the psalmist wrote about was what he had meditated on. Yes, his inmost feelings resulted in his words of praise; "his tongue is the pen of a ready writer." Is our tongue always ready to speak about the King our Lord from what we have meditated upon? In Matthew 12:34 Jesus said, "Out of the abundance of the heart the mouth speaks."

The psalmist's heart was bubbling over with what had been upon his mind about the king and his beauty, and he could hardly wait to put his thoughts into words to tell someone. I wonder if when we go out into the streets having meditated upon the Lord, we are keen to tell someone about Him.

In verse 2, the psalmist addressed the king with an impressive and wonderful description: "Thou art fairer than the children of men." I think of his description of the king in five aspects.

His physical beauty
His moral glory
His official glory
His divine glory (intrinsic and personal)
His garments

First, His physical beauty. We can recall what the prophet Isaiah said of Him. In Isaiah 53:2, we read, "As a root out of a dry ground: He hath no form nor comeliness; and when we shall see him, there is no beauty that we should desire him." And yet the psalmist can say, "Thou art fairer than the children of men." Is there a contradiction?

Beauty is a difficult attribute to describe. When I sat my A level examination in economics when I was in grammar school, one question was, "Beauty is in the eye of the beholder. Discuss this statement in relation to the subject of economics." I had never heard that phrase before, but I now know exactly what it means. It is the same idea expressed by Peter in 1 Peter 2:7: "Unto you therefore which believe He is precious." It is a subjective opinion ... to you who believe He is precious, but the corollary is true ... to you who do not believe He is not precious.

Yes, we can agree with the psalmist, "He is fairer than the sons of men." The word *fairer* should be better translated "fairer by far" or "fairer, fairer," or even "beautiful, beautiful."

Once, we saw no beauty in Him that we should desire Him, but now it is different. We know that physical beauty is only skin deep, but true beauty includes what is not seen, and that is what brings delight. "I was daily his [My Father's] delight" (Proverbs 8:30).

Jesus is described in the scriptures as the rose of Sharon and as the lily of the valley. He is altogether lovely. In Song of Songs 5:9, the question is asked of the bride, "What is thy beloved more than another beloved?" to which the bride responded, "He is altogether lovely" (5:16).

This passage also refers to His moral glory. "Grace is poured into Thy lips." I like the thought that grace was poured into His lips because during His time on earth, grace poured from His lips. We read in Luke 4:22, "[They] wondered at the gracious words which proceeded out of His mouth." "Jesus was full of grace and truth" (John 1:14). John also wrote, "Grace and truth came by Jesus Christ" (John 1:17).

Then there is His official glory (vv. 3–6): His throne, His scepter, His sword, and His horse. While on earth, He had no literal sword, scepter, throne, or war horse; His sword was the Word of God, and His scepter was the scepter of righteousness.

In Zechariah 9:9, we read,

Rejoice greatly, O daughter of Zion; shout, O
daughter of Jerusalem: behold, thy King cometh
unto thee: he is just, and having salvation; lowly,
and riding upon an ass, and upon a colt the foal
of an ass.

This prophecy was fulfilled in Matthew 21:1–11 when Jesus
rode on a donkey into Jerusalem. The day is coming when Jesus
will ride in majesty as King of Kings and Lord of Lords. What a
contrast! Instead of a meek and lowly king riding on a donkey,
He will be a stern King riding on a white charger to destroy his
enemies.

Jesus on a throne, the throne of grace. Hebrews 4:16 reads, "Let
us come therefore boldly unto the throne of grace, that we may
obtain mercy and find grace to help in time of need." But He also
wants us to set Him apart in our hearts, to sit on the thrones of our
hearts: "But sanctify the Lord God in your hearts" (1 Peter 3:15).

The throne reminds us of a future day when instead of the
throne of grace, He will sit on a great white throne of judgment
and judge all whose names are not written in the Lamb's Book
of Life. The Day of Grace will have come to an end. But the
psalmist talked of His throne as being an eternal throne. What
kind of throne will that be? John described the New Jerusalem in
Revelation 22:3–5 (TLB).

The throne of God and of the Lamb will be there,
and his servants will worship him. And they shall
see his face; and his name shall be written on their
foreheads. And there will be no night there—no
need for lamps or sun—for the Lord God will be
their light; and they shall reign forever and ever.

Finally, there is His divine glory, His personal glory. In verse
6, Jesus was addressed as God: "Thy throne, O God is for ever."

This refers to the personal glory of the Lord Jesus, the divine glory He had before the world was. In John 17:5, Jesus prayed, "Now, O Father, glorify thou me with thine own self with the glory which I had with thee before the world was."

His personal glory is His intrinsic glory, not a reflected glory. The writer of the letter to the Hebrews reminds us of this in Hebrews 1:2–3 where he spoke of Christ as the one "by whom he made the worlds, Who is the brightness of God's glory, and the express image of His person, and upholding all things by the word of His power."

His Garments

The psalmist also spoke of Christ's garments: "All thy garments smell of myrrh, aloes and cassia, out of the ivory palaces" (Psalm 45:8). Do these three spices have any lessons to teach us? Let us consider each one.

Myrrh was a costly perfume. It was one of the gifts brought by the wise men to Jesus, and it was one of the spices Nicodemus brought to the tomb for embalming the body of Jesus. Was this myrrh that perfumed the garments of the King in this psalm an omen, a prediction of the death of Christ some hundreds of years later?

> There came also Nicodemus, which at the first came to Jesus by night, and brought a mixture of myrrh and aloes, about an hundred-pound weight. Then took they the body of Jesus, and wound it in linen clothes with the spices, as the manner of the Jews is to bury. (John 19:39)

Similarly, aloes were costly spices used to embalm the body of Jesus. In Numbers 24:5–6 (RSV), we read about Balaam, who wanted to curse Israel, but in a vision, he saw how God would bless His people. Balaam saw the tents of the Israelites as a beautiful garden that included aloes God had planted.

How fair are your tents, O Jacob, your encampments, O Israel! Like valleys that stretch afar, like gardens beside a river, like aloes that the Lord has planted, like cedar trees beside the waters.

Cassia was a costly perfume that in Old Testament times was used in the tabernacle to add a beautiful scent to the garments of the high priest and to the furniture. "And thou shalt make holy garments for Aaron thy brother for glory and for beauty" (Exodus 28:2).

The Bible teaches that the tabernacle and the priest's garments were illustrations or copies of the true tabernacle and its priesthood. We read in Hebrews 9:11 that the Lord Jesus was greater than the temple and greater than Aaron: "But Christ being come a high priest of good things to come, by a greater and more perfect tabernacle, not made with hands."

O that we would draw close enough to Jesus that we might smell the sweetness of His garments!

5

Availing Prayer

Reading: James 5:16–18

> The effectual, fervent prayer of a righteous man availeth much. Elijah was a man subject to like passions as we are, and he prayed earnestly that it might not rain. And it rained not on the earth by the space of three years and six months. And he prayed again, and the heaven gave rain, and the earth brought forth her fruit.

Elijah was obviously a man of prayer. He was a righteous man whose prayers released power. The NIV states that "the prayer of a righteous man is powerful and effective."

James wrote these words to illustrate effective prayer (1 Kings 17–18). Wicked King Ahab and Jezebel, his queen, had led Israel away from the Lord and into the worship of Baal. God punished the nation by holding back the rain it needed (see Deuteronomy 28:12–24). For three and a half years, there was no rain.

Then Elijah challenged the priests of Baal on Mount Carmel. All day long, the priests cried out to their god, but no answer came. At the time of the evening sacrifice, Elijah repaired the altar and prepared the sacrifice. He prayed but once, and fire came down from heaven to consume the sacrifice. That was proof that Jehovah was the true God. However, the nation still needed rain. Elijah went to the top of Mount Carmel and fell down before the Lord in prayer. He prayed and sent his servant seven times to see if there was evidence of rain, and the seventh time, his servant saw a little cloud. Soon, the rains came, and the nation was saved.

Do we need showers of blessing today? We certainly do!

The world worships Baal and other false gods. Our churches are feeling the effects of it with closures and dwindling congregations. But we should take heart because Jesus said, "I will build my church and the gates of hell shall not prevail against it" (Matthew 16:18).

"But," you might argue, "Elijah was a special prophet of God. We can expect God to answer his prayers in a wonderful way. But who am I?"

There are three things to notice about Elijah: First, he was an ordinary man; his praying was something that could characterize us. We have the capacity to pray just as Elijah did, and our prayers can avail much. Elijah was a man just like us as stated in James (5:17): "a man subject to like passions as we are." He was not perfect; in fact, soon after his victory on Mount Carmel, he became afraid and discouraged and ran away.

In Luke 18:11–14, Jesus told the parable of the Pharisee and the publican who went to the temple to pray. You will recall the prayer of the Pharisee who said, "I thank Thee that I am not as other men are, or even as this publican." He thanked God that he was not like other men. The difference between Elijah and the Pharisee was that Elijah knew he was an ordinary man subject to his passions as we are, and just like us, he knew he was a sinner. The Pharisee was self-righteous and full of pride, and his prayer went no further than the ceiling. The Bible says that a humble and contrite heart God will not despise.

Second, Elijah was an obedient man. In 1 Kings 17:2, 5 we read,

> The word of the Lord came to him and said, Get thee hence to the brook Cherith. So, he went and did according unto the word of the Lord ... and again, the word of the Lord came to him and said, get thee to Zarephath, and he arose and went to Zarephath.

There was no questioning God as to why he should go; he simply went. I mention his obedience in relation to prayer because our verse says the effectual and fervent prayer refers to a righteous man.

It is the prayer of a righteous man that avails much. The word *righteous* has nothing to do with the righteousness imputed to us as believers when we first trusted Christ; the interpretation in this text means obedient to the Lord, living a life pleasing to the Lord, and trusting Him. The Hebrew word indicates that it means virtuous. We should beware because even though we have been made righteous by the blood of Christ, we may be disobedient to God's Word, and we may not be living lives that please Him. In that sense, we may not be righteous, and our prayers may therefore not avail much.

How can we expect the Lord to answer our prayers so that they avail much and have a great outcome if our lives are not what they should be because we are not obedient to His Word as we should be?

Third, Elijah was a trusting man. His prayers availed much because he had faith that God would control events. God told Elijah what His plans were, to send rain, and Elijah prayed that the Lord's will would be done. He trusted God to fulfill His Word.

"Prayer," said one Bible scholar, "is not getting man's will done in heaven. It's getting God's will done on earth." You cannot separate the Word of God and prayer, for in His Word, He gives us the promises we claim when we pray.

Elijah's prayers were fervent, frequent, and focused. He trusted God that the famine would come, and then he trusted God that the rain would come after more than three years of famine and drought. We need showers of blessing just like rain, and we must trust God to fulfill His purposes.

The rain is a picture of the victory of conversion, of revival, and of souls being saved. We should be praying that there will be a revival among us, that the famine will become showers of blessing. Elijah was not only believing in his praying; he was also persistent: "He prayed and he prayed again" (James 5:17–18). On Mount Carmel, Elijah continued to pray for rain until his servant reported, "Behold, there ariseth a little cloud out of the sea, like a man's hand" (1 Kings 18:44).

Many times, we fail to get what God promises because we stop praying. The Bible tells us in Matthew 6:7 that we are not heard for our much praying. There is, however, a difference between our vain repetitions and true believing persistence in prayer. We know that Jesus prayed three times in the Garden of Gethsemane and that Paul prayed three times that his thorn in the flesh might be taken from him.

Elijah was determined and concerned in his praying. "He prayed earnestly" (James 5:17 NIV). The literal Greek reads "and he prayed in prayer." Many people do not pray in their prayers. Often, when we pray, we fall into the habit of repeating the same phrases we have often used as a matter of routine, and there does not seem to be any fervency, reality, or expectancy in our prayers. How often have you heard the saying, "He says his prayers, but he does not pray?"

A Christian who attended a prayer meeting faithfully always said the same things when he prayed. His prayer was seldom varied: "O Lord, thank you that the doors of this church are always open for people to come in." Eventually, another brother, remembering the commission of the Lord Jesus to go into all the world, interjected and shouted, "and thank you that the doors are open so that we can go out!"

There are other instances in the life of Elijah when he displayed confidence and trust that the Lord would perform a miracle. One was when he needed food, and he met a widow who had only a handful of meal, barley or oats, and a small jar of oil. Yet Elijah asked her for some of it believing that God would do a miracle with the widow's handful of meal and a little oil. We should be trusting the Lord to supply all our needs.

And again, he trusted God that He would raise the widow's son to life again reminding us that everlasting life is what we proclaim in the gospel, and we should be praying that souls dead in trespasses and sins will have eternal life through faith in Christ.

He trusted God that He would bring fire from heaven to consume the sacrifice when the 450 prophets of Baal had failed to get any response from their false god thus proving that Jehovah was the true God and reminding us that by frequent and focused prayer the powers of darkness can be overcome. This is how Elijah's prayers availed much.

Devout believers often fail to take seriously the promises of God contained in the scriptures in practical everyday living. For example, Paul told the Philippians (4:19), "My God shall supply all your need according to his riches in glory by Christ Jesus."

What is believing prayer? Imagine praying for rain during a drought and then going outside without an umbrella. It serves you right if you get soaked. Did you not believe God would answer your prayer?

Prayer power is the greatest power in the world today. History shows how humankind has progressed from manpower to horsepower, then to TNT and dynamite, and to atomic power, and now to nuclear power. But greater than nuclear power is the power of prayer. Elijah prayed for his nation, and God answered his prayer. We need to pray for our nation that God will bring conviction and revival and that showers of blessing will come to the land. One of the first responsibilities of the church is to pray for government leaders (1 Timothy 2:1–3).

One of my favorite verses in the Bible is 2 Chronicles 7:14. At the dedication of Solomon's temple, the Lord said to Solomon,

> If my people, which are called by my name, shall humble themselves, and pray, and seek my face, and turn from their wicked ways; then will I hear from heaven, and will forgive their sin, and will heal their land.

Do we know what is the difference between praying and seeking God's face? We read in Psalm 27:8 that King David had evidently heard God saying, "Seek my face," and he responded, "When thou saidst, seek ye my face; my heart said unto thee, Thy face, Lord, will I seek."

God never intended that His people should pray to Him as strangers. He wants us to draw near to Him just as children go to a loving father to seek His face to obtain His favor. In Old Testament times, when a man prostrated himself before his master to make a request, his superior would raise the supplicant's head as a sign that the favor would be granted.

To look someone in the eye is to test whether they are sincere. If you question others about their behavior, it is a sure sign that they are not telling the truth if they do not look you in the eye. I'm not suggesting that is the reason the Lord wants us to seek His face, but it may well be to receive from Him the favor of granting our request. May we all be like Elijah, ordinary people but fervent and effective in prayer.

Here are some words of comfort from Job 19:25–27 (NLT).

But as for me, I know that my Redeemer lives, and he will stand upon the earth at last. And after my body has decayed, yet in my body I will see God! I will see him for myself. Yes, I will see him with my own eyes. I am overwhelmed at the thought!

6

Honor Him

Reading: **1 Samuel 2:30**

Them that honour Me I will honour.

In his letter to the church in Rome, Paul encouraged the believers to "Be kindly affectioned one to another with brotherly love; in honour preferring one another" (Romans 12:10). And Exodus 20:12 tells us, "Honour thy father and thy mother that thy days may be long upon the land which the Lord thy God giveth thee."

Times have changed since I was a schoolboy. Then, we would show respect to our teachers, policemen, doctors, and many others because they were servants of the community, but in the present, people seem to have lost some of that respect for them.

Yet all is not lost; every year at eleven in the morning on the eleventh day of November, Remembrance Day is observed; the country stops for one minute to remember and honor the many men and women in the armed forces who died in action to save their country. The practice began when World War I ended at eleven in the morning on the eleventh day of the eleventh month.

I think the young people today still understand the great sacrifices that were made.

Throughout history, monarchs have rewarded with gifts or titles those who have shown them service, loyalty, or gallantry. After medieval times, physical gifts such as land or money were replaced by the awarding of knighthoods and of membership in orders of chivalry accompanied by insignia such as gold or silver chains and medals.

Until the beginning of the nineteenth century, only members of the upper class and high-ranking military figures could be appointed to an order of chivalry, but later, appointments were drawn from a wider variety of backgrounds.

In 1917, the queen's grandfather, King George V, developed a new order of chivalry, the Order of the British Empire (OBE), as a way of rewarding men and women who had made an outstanding contribution to the war effort. Nowadays, the OBE rewards service in a wide range of areas from acting to charity work with honors that include the well-known MBE and CBE.

Queen Elizabeth II has the sole right of conferring titles of honor on deserving people from all walks of life in public recognition of their merit, service, loyalty, or bravery in the UK and the Commonwealth. This usually happens twice a year. One of the occasions is when deserving people are listed on the Queen's Birthday Honours List.

The story is told in the Old Testament's book Esther of Mordecai, a man who honored the king and who was honored by the king in return for his services. The king of Persia, Xerxes, chose a new queen, Esther, an orphan Jew, the adopted daughter of a minor court official named Mordecai.

The book tells of Haman, a court official who thought he had been slighted by Mordecai and sought revenge. He wanted not only Mordecai but also all the Jews there exterminated. When Haman asked Xerxes for permission for that, the king granted it.

But Mordecai had earlier warned the king of a plot on his life, and somehow, his reward had been overlooked. One night, Xerxes could not sleep, and he had the record, the diary of his rule, read. The fact that Mordecai had saved the king's life by revealing the plot to kill him was there in the record, but there was no mention of a reward. We read this in Esther 6:4–11 (NKJV).

Now Haman came into the court of the king's palace, to speak to the king about hanging Mordecai on the gallows that he had prepared for him. So, Haman came in, and the king asked him, What shall be done for the man whom the king delights to honour?

Now Haman thought in his heart, Whom would the king delight to honour more than me? And Haman answered the king, For the man whom the king delights to honour, let a royal robe be brought which the king has worn, and a horse on which the king has ridden, which has a royal crest placed on its head. Then let this robe and horse be delivered to the hand of one of the king's most noble princes, that he may array the man whom the king delights to honour. Then parade him on horseback through the city square and proclaim before him: Thus shall it be done to the man whom the king delights to honour!

Then the king said to Haman, Hurry, take the robe and the horse, as you have suggested, and do so for Mordecai the Jew who sits within the king's gate! Leave nothing undone of all that you have spoken.

What a shock for Haman who was expecting the king to honour him!

> So, Haman took the robe and the horse, arrayed Mordecai, and led him on horseback through the city square, and proclaimed before him, Thus shall it be done to the man whom the king delights to honour.
>
> When one of the king's servants volunteered that Haman had already had gallows erected on which to hang Mordecai, whom the king had ordered him to honour, Xerxes had Haman and his sons hanged there instead. (NKJV)

I am reminded of one who was not saved from the gallows and because of His pleasing the Father was highly honored by Him.

As Jesus hung on the cross, the psalmist in Psalm 22:7–8 portrayed Jesus as the victim of suffering and death.

> All they that see me laugh me to scorn: they shoot out the lip, they shake the head saying, He trusted on the Lord that he would deliver Him: let Him deliver Him, seeing he delighted in Him.

The glorious truth is that Jesus was delivered and raised back to life. In Acts 5:30–31, we read,

> The God of our fathers raised up Jesus, whom ye slew and hanged on a tree. Him hath God exalted with his right hand to be a Prince and a Saviour, for to give repentance to Israel, and forgiveness of sins.

What a wonderful Savior we have! By His mercy and grace, He ordained that those who truly loved and served Him would be rewarded; 1 Peter 1:4–9 (TLB) reads,

> And God has reserved for his children the priceless gift of eternal life; it is kept in heaven for you, pure and undefiled, beyond the reach of change and decay. And God, in his mighty power, will make sure that you get there safely to receive it because you are trusting him. It will be yours in that coming last day for all to see. So be truly glad! There is wonderful joy ahead, even though the going is rough for a while down here.
>
> These trials are only to test your faith, to see whether or not it is strong and pure. It is being tested as fire tests gold and purifies it—and your faith is far more precious to God than mere gold; so, if your faith remains strong after being tried in the test tube of fiery trials, it will bring you much praise and glory and honour on the day of his return.
>
> You love him even though you have never seen him; though not seeing him, you trust him; and even now you are happy with the inexpressible joy that comes from heaven itself. And your further reward for trusting him will be the salvation of your souls.

My Portion

7

When I was a child, my father and grandfather had a garden allotment they tended at least once a week. My father would mark out with string some of the allotment for my brother and me so we could also plant and water seeds and watch lettuce and other vegetables grow. And boy, did we enjoy our regular visits to see how the plants were growing.

Psalm 16 (ESV), written by David during his exile, is sometimes called the golden psalm because it contains a treasure. It reminds me of my childhood days in the garden.

> The Lord is my chosen portion and my cup; you hold my lot. The lines have fallen for me in pleasant places; indeed, I have a beautiful inheritance.

> I bless the Lord who gives me counsel; in the night also, my heart instructs me. I have set the Lord always before me because he is at my right hand, I shall not be shaken.

Therefore, my heart is glad, and my whole being rejoices; my flesh also dwells secure. For you will not abandon my soul to Sheol or let your holy one see corruption.

You make known to me the path of life; in your presence there is fullness of joy; at your right hand are pleasures forevermore.

The words *my portion* and *my lot* could be translated as "my allotment," "my inheritance," and the *lines* could be translated as "the cords."

The Lord is my chosen inheritance as He was David's. It was my choice to make Him my portion, and I could not have made a better choice. In this psalm, we see the Lord Jesus in prophecy.

To possess great wealth but not have the Lord is poverty (Luke 12:13–21), and to enjoy the gifts but ignore the giver is foolishness. If Jesus is the Lord of our lives, our possessions and circumstances represent the inheritance He gives us. But there is more; we have an eternal inheritance.

The Israelites longed for the Promised Land ever since God promised it to them on several occasions to Abraham, Jacob, and Moses (Genesis 28:13–14; Exodus 3:17). It was to be their inheritance and allotted to the twelve tribes apart from the tribe of Levi: Joshua 11:23 (ESV) reads,

> So, Joshua took the whole land, according to all that the Lord said unto Moses; and Joshua gave it for an inheritance unto Israel according to their divisions by their tribes.

> But the tribe of Levi was not to have a portion of the land, even as Aaron had already been

told, because the Lord was to be their portion.
(Deuteronomy 10:8–9)

> At that time the Lord set apart the tribe of Levi to
> carry the ark of the covenant of the Lord to stand
> before the Lord to minister to him and to bless
> in his name, to this day. Therefore, Levi has no
> portion or inheritance with his brothers. The Lord
> is his inheritance [portion], as the Lord your God
> said to him.

But the Lord did not forget the Levites; He gave them the tithe offerings. Numbers 18:21 (ASV) reads,

> And unto the children of Levi, behold, I have
> given all the tithe in Israel for an inheritance, in
> return for their service which they serve, even the
> service of the tent of meeting [the tabernacle].

They were to have no inheritance of land because God was to be their portion, their inheritance. Those who have God as their inheritance ought not look on or covet the world and its transient pleasures.

Even Abraham was looking for something more than land, something more durable.

> By faith Abraham obeyed when he was called
> to go out to a place that he was to receive as an
> inheritance. And he went out, not knowing where
> he was going. By faith he went to live in the land
> of promise, as in a foreign land, living in tents
> with Isaac and Jacob, heirs with him of the same
> promise. For he was looking forward to the city

that has foundations, whose builder and maker is God. (Hebrews 11:8–10 ESV)

What wonderful words of Jeremiah in Lamentations 3:24: "The Lord is my portion, saith my soul; therefore, will I hope in him." We can rest in those words.

We often think in terms of our earthly inheritance. In this world, the lines have fallen to us in good places, but surely, we have a more permanent inheritance than this world can offer.

Blessed be the God and Father of our Lord Jesus Christ! According to his great mercy, He has caused us to be born again to a living hope through the resurrection of Jesus Christ from the dead to an inheritance that is imperishable, undefiled, and unfading, kept in heaven for you. (1 Peter 1:3–4 ESV).

In 1 John 2:15–17, we read,

Love not the world, neither the things that are in the world. If any man love the world, the love of the Father is not in him. For all that is in the world, the lust of the flesh, and the lust of the eyes, and the pride of life, is not of the Father, but is of the world. And the world passeth away, and the lust thereof; but he that doeth the will of God abideth for ever.

In Matthew 6:25–34 (TLB), Jesus said,

So, my counsel is: Don't worry about things— food, drink, and clothes. For you already have life and a body and they are far more important than

what to eat and wear. Look at the birds! They
don't worry about what to eat; they don't need
to sow or reap or store up food, for your heavenly
Father feeds them. And you are far more valuable
to him than they are. Will all your worries add a
single moment to your life? And why worry about
your clothes? Look at the field of lilies! They don't
worry about theirs. Yet King Solomon in all his
glory was not clothed as beautifully as they. And if
God cares so wonderfully for flowers that are here
today and gone tomorrow, won't he more surely
care for you, O men of little faith?

So don't worry at all about having enough food
and clothing. Why be like the heathen? For
they take pride in all these things and are deeply
concerned about them. But your heavenly Father
already knows perfectly well that you need them,
and he will give them to you if you give him first
place in your life and live as he wants you to. So
don't be anxious about tomorrow. God will take
care of your tomorrow too. Live one day at a time.

It is interesting to know that the Lord has His portion too. We
read in Deuteronomy 32:9–11 (ESV),

The Lord's portion is His people, Jacob His
allotted heritage. He found him in a desert land,
and in the howling waste of the wilderness; He
encircled him, He cared for him, He kept him
as the apple of His eye. Like an eagle that stirs
up its nest, that flutters over its young, spreading
out its wings, catching them, bearing them on its
pinions.

In 1 Peter 2:9–10 (ESV), we read,

> But you are a chosen race, a royal priesthood, a holy nation, a people for His own possession, that you may proclaim the excellencies of Him who called you out of darkness into his marvellous light. Once you were not a people, but now you are God's people; once you had not received mercy, but now you have received mercy.

Psalm 16:5 tells us we have many privileges one of which is that our inheritance is secure. "Thou maintainest my lot" means "You will not suffer any one to dispossess me of this my lot," not like earthly possessions, which are sometimes stolen or taken away from the lawful owner.

> Bless the Lord, O my soul, and all that is within me, bless His holy Name. (Psalm 103:1)

Approval

8

If we are looking for something reliable and of quality when we go shopping, we look for items that have the approval of some known authority to avoid buying a substandard item. In Acts 2:22–24, we read of a man who was approved by God.

> Ye men of Israel, hear these words; Jesus of Nazareth, a man approved of God among you by miracles and wonders and signs, which God did by him in the midst of you, as ye yourselves also know: Him, being delivered by the determinate counsel and foreknowledge of God, ye have taken, and by wicked hands have crucified and slain: Whom God hath raised up, having loosed the pains of death, because it was not possible that he should be holden of it.

We can break these verses down into several headings.

Jesus of Nazareth

There was a stigma attached to the description "Jesus of Nazareth" because surrounding towns held Nazareth in scorn. Nathanael asked Philip, "Can there any good thing come out of Nazareth?" (John 1:46). I like Philip's reply: "Come and see."

What condescension and humility characterized the Lord Jesus to think that He, the Son of God, "was in the world, and the world was made through him, yet the world did not know him. That He came to his own, and his own people did not receive him" (John 1:10–11 ESV).

Jesus the Man

Jesus, the Son of God, became a man just like us apart from sin.

Hebrews 4:15, reads, "For we have not a high priest which cannot be touched with the feeling of our infirmities; but was in all points tempted [tested] like as we are, yet without sin." Jesus knew what it was to be tired, to weep, to be compassionate, to hunger, and to thirst. He knew poverty having been born in a manger.

The Man Approved of God

Adam was the first man, but he failed God. Paul explained in 1 Corinthians 15:21–22, "For since by man [Adam] came death, by man [Jesus] also came the resurrection of the dead. For as in Adam all die, even so in Christ shall all be made alive." In 1 Corinthians 15:47, he wrote, "The first man is of the earth, earthy: the second man is the Lord from heaven." The first man failed, but God in His grace sent His Son as the second man, who was approved by God.

When the Lord Jesus walked on this scene, He had the mark of God's approval, not man's approval; indeed, they rejected Him though He met God's perfect standards.

We read in John 8:29 that Jesus said, "I do always those things that please him [the Father]." God testified to this when He opened the heavens more than once to declare that Jesus was His beloved Son in whom He was well pleased.

We should always strive to be approved by God. We are not talking about salvation. We know that we belong to Him and are accepted in the Beloved One; our salvation depends on the redemptive work of Christ on the cross, not on our efforts. But now that we are saved, we should want to please the Lord.

The Christian ambition is expressed in 2 Corinthians 5:9: "Wherefore, we labour that we may be accepted of Him [that we may be well-pleasing to Him]."

The Man Appointed by God

Acts 2:23 reads, "Him, being delivered by the determinate counsel and foreknowledge of God, ye have taken, and by wicked hands have crucified and slain."

The phrase "determinate counsel and foreknowledge of God" means "by appointment of God." God planned for Jesus, the appointed Lamb of God "slain from the foundation of the world" (Revelation 13:8) to be crucified. Even the time of His death had been appointed. Jesus was always in the will of His Father; nothing happened to Him by chance.

The Ascended Man

Jesus was the man "whom God hath raised up, having loosed the pains of death: because it was not possible that he should be holden of it" (Acts 2:24). Yes, He was the resurrected man for death could not hold Him, but later, He ascended back to His Father to receive glory and honor.

How can we obtain God's stamp of approval? The Bible gives us several indications.

By Walking in the Light

Ephesians 5:8–10 reads, "Walk as children of light: For the fruit of the Spirit is in all goodness and righteousness and truth; proving what is acceptable unto the Lord." We are to learn what pleases Him and demonstrate the fruits of the Spirit—love, joy, peace, long-suffering, gentleness, goodness, faith, meekness, and temperance.

By Serving God Acceptably with Reverence and Godly Fear

"Let us have grace, whereby we may serve God acceptably with reverence and godly fear" (Hebrews 12:28). The Amplified New Testament puts it like this: "Let us therefore offer to God pleasing service and acceptable worship, with modesty and pious care and godly fear and awe."

By Studying the Scriptures

"Study to show thyself approved unto God, a workman that needeth not to be ashamed, rightly dividing the word of truth" (2 Timothy 2:15).

And the ultimate way of being approved by God is in Romans 12:1 (RSV): "to present your bodies as a living sacrifice, holy and acceptable to God, which is your spiritual worship."

We want to live lives that are approved by God, but we need to remember 2 Corinthians 10:18 (NKJV): "For not he that commends himself is approved, but whom the Lord commends."

9

God Can Meet All Our Needs

Reading: Philippians 4:19

> My God shall supply all your need according to
> His riches in glory by Christ Jesus.

The Lord's earthly life was driven by others' needs. That's not quite true, because He was driven by a greater motivation—to do His Father's will—but that included meeting the needs of everyone He encountered. And He came to meet the needs of the world, the reason He died on the cross and rose again.

Mark's gospel portrays Jesus as God's perfect servant, the key verse being 10:45 (NKJV): "For even the Son of Man did not come to be served, but to serve, and to give His life a ransom for many."

In answer to His critics who complained that He ate and drank with publicans and sinners, Jesus said, "Those who are well have no need of a physician, but those who are sick. I have not come to call the righteous, but sinners, to repentance" (Luke 5:31–32 NKJV).

You remember how even as a young boy of about twelve,

He told Joseph and Mary, "Wist ye not that I must be about My Father's business" (Luke 2:49).

He served God first and then served others. He was motivated by compassion for those desperately in need. The gospel records are full of cases where Jesus met people's needs, not just the needs of the multitudes but also of individuals.

He wept over the city of Jerusalem because people there did not recognize their need of Him as their Savior. He came unto His own, but His own received Him not.

When the four friends brought the palsied man to Jesus, His first words were, "Son, thy sins be forgiven thee." The man needed physical healing, but Jesus dealt with his greater need, and after that, he healed his physical ills.

The woman of Samaria had needs greater than fetching water, and Jesus made a detour to go through Samaria to meet her spiritual need for the Living Water.

At the wedding of Cana, the host was faced with the embarrassing shortage of wine, and Jesus met that need by changing water into the best wine.

Jesus calmed the storm on the Sea of Galilee for His disciples' sake, He exorcized the demons tormenting the possessed man in Gadara, and He met the needs of many others during His ministry on earth.

Just as He did then, Jesus can meet our every need. Matthew 6:9 (NKJV) says, "Your Father knows the things you have need of before you ask Him."

In Luke 12:27–31 (NKJV), we read,

> Consider the lilies, how they grow: they neither toil nor spin; and yet I say to you, even Solomon in all his glory was not arrayed like one of these. If then God so clothes the grass, which today is in the field and tomorrow is thrown into the oven,

how much more will He clothe you, O you of little faith?

And do not seek what you should eat or what you should drink, nor have an anxious mind. For all these things the nations of the world seek after, and your Father knows that you need these things. But seek the kingdom of God, and all these things shall be added to you.

We have already quoted Philippians 4:19.

My God shall supply all your need according to His riches in glory by Christ Jesus.

My mind was triggered to think of this verse when studying Paul's letter to the Ephesians. We have some interesting phrases beginning with "according to the riches." In Ephesians 1:7, we have "the forgiveness of sins according to the riches of His grace." In Ephesians 3:16, Paul prayed that the Ephesian believers would be strengthened by might in the inner man "according to the riches of His glory." And here in our text verse, Philippians 4:19, we have the phrase, not "the riches of His glory" but "His riches *in* glory" (emphasis added). The bank vaults are in heaven.

D. L. Moody said that Philippians 4:19 was God's blank check for believers.

- The company, the drawer of the check is "My God"
- The promise is "shall supply"
- The amount is "all your needs"
- The account is "according to His riches in glory"
- The signer is "Christ Jesus"

Do we properly appreciate God's riches in glory? Do we pray as though we are asking the impossible of God? Are we conservative (small *c*) in the things we pray for? As a friend in Staffordshire often reminded us, "The Lord is not impoverished by giving." He has endless supplies. He sustained Elijah through the brook and through the ravens and eventually through the widow of Zarephath, and in the latter case, a supply of cake meal and oil for the woman that lasted throughout a drought.

I would remind you, however, that Elijah and the widow displayed obedience and faith in God. Has not God met our needs in Christ so far, and our greatest need at that, and at the greatest cost to Himself? Can He not therefore meet our every need? "Is anything too hard for the Lord?" (Genesis 18:14).

The purpose of this meditation is to encourage you in your prayer life to ask big things of the Lord. There are those in our fellowships with big needs, and I mean bigger than we can imagine—They have broken hearts, broken health, broken families, problems that seem to have no solutions, and severe pains physical and mental. We should be specific in our requests to the Lord and include their needs. Hebrews 4:15–16 reads,

> We have not an high priest which cannot be touched with the feeling of our infirmities … Let us therefore come boldly unto the throne of grace, that we may obtain mercy and find grace to help *in time of need* (emphasis added).

We are responsible for supplying the needs of our fellow believers, as John, the apostle of love, exhorted us to do: "But whoever has this world's goods, and sees his brother in need, and shuts up his heart from him, how does the love of God abide in him?" (1 John 3:17 NKJV).

Despair and Hope

10

In 1979, on the steps of Number 10 Downing Street, Margaret Thatcher, prime minister, quoted from the prayer of St. Francis of Assisi.

Where there is discord, may we bring harmony. Where there is error, may we bring truth. Where there is doubt, may we bring faith. And where there is despair, may we bring hope.

I want to talk about despair and hope. Millions of people are in despair. In Paul's letter to the church at Ephesus, he described them before they were saved as "having no hope and without God in the world" (Ephesians 2:12) and in Hebrews 2:15 as those "who through fear of death were all their lifetime subject to bondage."

Many Christians are suffering for their faith, being persecuted, and facing starvation, torture, and death, and others are suffering from ill health, infirmity, and other problems.

Some who are suffering lose hope and ask, "Why's this happening to me?" but Romans 8:28 tells us, "And we know that all things work together for good to them that love God, to them who are the called according to his purpose." The fact is that the Lord knows what is best for us even though we cannot understand it. A poem by Corrie ten Boom likens our lives to woven cloth; we cannot understand God's working out the pattern of our lives, and sometimes, we can see only the reverse side of the tapestry—a jumble of supposedly haphazard stitches—but God sees the other side, which is much more beautiful. His thoughts and ways are far above ours.

In his tribute to Prince Philip, duke of Edinburgh, the archbishop of Canterbury said very poignantly, "Grief is the price of love." He was referring to his happy seventy-three-year marriage to the queen. She is now grieving for the loss of the one she loved. That is the price of love.

We are reminded of the Savior's love for the world, which led to grief. Isaiah reminds us of the prophecy concerning the coming of the Christ: "He is despised and rejected of men; a man of sorrows and acquainted with grief" (Isaiah 53:3).

Despair is the opposite of hope. Circumstances can press in around us to the extent that we cannot see a way out, and that can lead to despair, but we are not to despair. I do not believe the queen is in despair because I believe she has a strong faith in the Lord. And certainly, Jesus did not despair because He knew He would rise on the third day.

For the believer, there should never be a cause for despair. Though circumstances seem to be against us, and we face all sorts of troubles whether financial, familial, or job related, we should never despair.

Paul coped with hopeless situations. He wrote in 2 Corinthians 4:8 (NIV), "We are hard pressed on every side, but not crushed; perplexed, but not in despair." He also wrote in Romans 8:18, "For I reckon that the sufferings of this present time are not worthy to be compared with the glory which shall be revealed in us." These surely are words of comfort.

Do you sometimes talk to yourself? I do. I have said to myself,

You silly boy! If we despair, Psalm 43:5 (NIV) gives us a model of how to talk to ourselves to pull ourselves together: "Why, my soul, are you downcast? Why so disturbed within me? Put your hope in God, for I will yet praise Him, my Saviour and my God."

Most people understand hope as wishful thinking as in "I hope [this or that] will happen" or "I hope it won't rain today" or "I hope my car will start." That is the world's definition of hope, but it is not the believer's definition. The biblical definition of hope is "confident expectation." In Romans 8:19, hope is referred to as our "earnest expectation."

Hebrews 6:18–19 describes the believers as those who

> have fled for refuge to lay hold upon the hope set before us: Which hope we have as an anchor of the soul, both sure and steadfast, and which entereth into that within the veil.

In Lamentations 3:1–18 (NKJV) are metaphors describing how Jeremiah had been afflicted by God for his sin and failure. In verse 18, he concluded that "My strength and my hope have perished from the Lord." He was in despair. But then in verses 19–24, his despair was turned into hope as he remembered, "Through the Lord's mercies we are not consumed; because His compassions fail not; they are new every morning; great is Thy faithfulness."

The confidence of Jeremiah is this in Lamentation 3:24 (NKJV): "The Lord is my portion says my soul; therefore, I hope in Him!"

The Bible contains numerous examples of people who were in hopeless situations. Just think of the woman with the hemorrhage of blood in Matthew 9:18–22 and Mark 5. She must have been in despair of ever being healed. She had suffered from the illness for twelve years and had seen many doctors none of whom had been able to cure her. Her illness had impoverished her. And when it seemed that this was her last opportunity to speak to Jesus, the

Great Physician, there was such a crowd around Him that the best she could do was to touch the hem of His garment. Though she was a desperate woman, her despair turned to hope. Jesus gave the answer. It was the woman's faith in Jesus.

In Matthew 9:21–22 we read,

> She said within herself, If I may but touch his garment, I shall be whole. But Jesus turned him about, and when he saw her, he said, Daughter, be of good comfort; thy faith hath made thee whole. And the woman was made whole from that hour.
>
> Now the God of hope fill you with all joy and peace in believing, that ye may abound in hope, through the power of the Holy Ghost. (Romans 15:13)

11

Attitudes to the Cross

Reading: Matthew 27:35–40

> And they crucified him, and parted his garments,
> casting lots that it might be fulfilled which was
> spoken by the prophet, they parted my garments
> among them, and upon my vesture did they cast
> lots. And sitting down they watched him there;
> and set up over his head his accusation written,
> This is Jesus the King of the Jews!
>
> Then were there two thieves crucified with him,
> one on the right hand, and another on the left.
> And they that passed by reviled him, wagging
> their heads, and saying, Thou that destroyest the
> temple, and buildest it in three days, save thyself.
> If thou be the Son of God, come down from the
> cross.

Many of those who witnessed Jesus's crucifixion were apathetic
and antagonistic, but others had an allegiance to Him.

Apathy

I attended a bullfight in Spain years ago. Spectators watched as the picadors and the matadors brutally tormented the innocent bull. When it was cruelly killed, the crowd roared its approval. They did not care about animal welfare. They sat there with their lunch boxes and drinks. I imagine this was the scene around the cross of Jesus. Matthew wrote in 27:36, "Sitting down they watched Him there."

Who were sitting down and watching Jesus die? Yes, the soldiers, the authorities, the religious leaders, but most likely, also ordinary people like you and me. Possibly, they had brought sandwiches for a picnic lunch; for many, the spectacle of an innocent man being tortured and killed was entertainment.

A teacher once asked a student the meaning of the word *apathy*. The student replied, "I don't know, and I don't care." "Well done," the teacher said. It means not caring, not interested. The apathetic display a "couldn't care less" attitude; apathy is another word for complacency.

People tend to be more concerned about physical and material things than with spiritual and eternal things. They are not aware that Jesus posed the rhetorical question, "What shall it profit a man if he shall gain the whole world and lose his own soul?" (Mark 8:36). If you examine yourself right now, I'm sure you would say, "Well, that's not my attitude!"

I am pretty sure that if those who couldn't care less about Jesus dying on the cross realized who Jesus was—the King of glory, the great Creator and upholder of all things— they would have acted differently.

Those of us who have watched in our imagination the suffering Savior on the cross would have had a response similar to that of Barabbas. Perhaps he was there sitting and watching and thinking, *Jesus died for me. He took my place. I should have been on that center cross!*

Antagonism

The second statement that describes people's attitude to the cross is in Matthew 27:39: "They that passed by ..." Jeremiah, writing hundreds of years before Christ, wrote a prophetic statement about Jesus on the cross.

> Is it nothing to you, all ye that pass by? behold, and see if there be any sorrow like unto my sorrow, which is done unto me, wherewith the Lord hath afflicted me in the day of his fierce anger. (Lamentations 1:12)

That was not apathy; it was antagonism and hatred toward Jesus. Matthew 7:39 reads, "And they that passed by reviled him, wagging their heads."

Nothing has really changed. For generations, many have ignored and even persecuted Christians, something Jesus had warned His disciples of (John 15:18).

Jesus's crucifixion was a climactic day; it was the day of God's judgment, when Jesus bore our sins in His body on the cross. But it was also a great day of victory because when Jesus cried out, "It is finished," He was declaring that He had completed the work of atonement and reconciliation and that God would be a just God as well as a Savior able to forgive and cleanse sinners who repented and trusted in the Savior.

But despite the magnitude of the momentous event taking place before their eyes, many people passed by too busy with their affairs, and others expressed antagonism to the man on the cross. We read in Mark 15:29 (NIV), "Those who passed by hurled insults at Him." Psalm 22:7 reads, "All they that see me laugh me to scorn; they shoot out the lip; they wag their heads." We find people doing the same today—using the name of Christ as a swear word.

Allegiance

There was a third attitude some displayed that day—allegiance, the attitude of subjects to their sovereign. "Now there stood by the cross of Jesus his mother, his mother's sister, Mary the wife of Cleophas, and Mary Magdalene" (John 19:25). They were there out of love and devotion.

I thank God that "the blest Man of Calvary has won my heart from me and died to set me free. Blest Man of Calvary." (quoting from an old hymn 'Fairest of all the earth beside' by M P Ferguson. Copyright is Public Domain).

Not many expressed their allegiance to Jesus that day, but one person who did was the repentant thief being crucified alongside Him. He took part in the conversation on the cross between the three victims.

In Matthew 27, we read that those who passed by reviled Him, wagging their heads. They also challenged Jesus as to His deity: verse 4 reads, "If thou be the Son of God, come down from the cross." And verse 44 tells us, "The thieves also which were crucified with Him cast the same in his teeth!"

A soul-searching conversation commenced between the two criminals. The one rebuked the other saying, "Don't you fear God? We are all in the same position, except that we both deserve our punishment whereas this man [Jesus] has done nothing wrong."

That was when he said to Jesus, "Lord, remember me when you come into your kingdom." His faith in Christ was displayed as he recognized Jesus as the Son of God, the Lord with a kingdom. He recognized that he needed God's forgiveness, and he clinched his salvation by asking the Lord to remember him.

Consider the Roman centurion who witnessed the crucifixion. Can you imagine the turmoil going on in his mind as he witnessed the suffering which Jesus endured and then felt the earthquake and watched the sky turn dark for three hours in the middle of the day? His conscience must have made him realize that Jesus was no ordinary man. He had never seen events like that before though no doubt he had witnessed many crucifixions, but he knew this one was different. I think he was touched by the response of Jesus to all that was happening to Him. Here was the King of the Jews exhibiting majestic sweetness.

The centurion saw Jesus's brow pierced by a crown of thorns, the brow that only the night before had sweat as it were great drops of blood in the Garden of Gethsemane. Just as the piercing eyes of Jesus had caused Peter to weep when he realized the enormity of his failure in denying his Lord, I wonder if the centurion's eyes met with the suffering Savior's eyes? Did he see hatred and revenge in them? No. He looked into the face of this one near death above whose head was placed the title King of the Jews, and he must have thought, *This is no carpenter.* The centurion's response was the correct one: "Truly this was the Son of God" (Matthew 27:54).

12

Girdles

In John 5:39, Jesus told His disciples, "Search the scriptures, for they are they which testify of Me." In Luke 24:27, we read that in His conversation with the two on the road to Emmaus, "beginning at Moses and all the prophets, He [Jesus] expounded unto them in all the scriptures the things concerning Himself."

Very often, events recorded in the Bible that took place with real people were also figures, types, or illustrations of events that would take place many years later, sometimes even thousands of years later, and very often pointed to Christ.

For example, there are references to the lamb in the Old Testament. The lamb was also a type or figure of the Lord Jesus, who was described by John the Baptist as "the Lamb of God." And in his first letter 1:18–19, Peter also described Jesus as a lamb.

> For as much as ye know that ye were not redeemed with corruptible things, as silver and gold, from your vain conversation received by tradition from your fathers, but with the precious blood of Christ, as of a lamb without blemish and without spot.

The tabernacle was an illustration or type of Christ with all its furniture. Even the high priest spoke of Christ, our great High Priest. Hebrews 9:24 (NLT) tells us,

> For Christ did not enter into a holy place made with human hands, which was only a copy of the true one in heaven. He entered into heaven itself to appear now before God on our behalf.

Moses penned the first five books of the Old Testament, which contain forty-six chapters devoted to the tabernacle and the priestly functions. These chapters speak of and testify to Jesus.

Every part of the priest's garment was important because they were for glory and beauty of the office of priest. The garments of the high priest speak of the glories of Christ. The high priest had some wonderful garments such as a plain coat of fine linen speaking of the humanity of Christ. Over that came the robe of the ephod, which was blue and also made of fine linen. It was interwoven on the hem with pomegranates of blue, purple, and scarlet with bells of gold. This would speak of the glories of Christ as the Son of man and the Son of God.

Then there was the ephod, again embroidered with colors of gold, blue, purple, and scarlet, and set on the shoulders were two onyx stones on which the names of the twelve tribes of Israel were engraved. There were other garments, and figuratively, they all spoke of the glories and beauties of Christ.

The Girdle

I want to consider one part of the high priest's garments in particular—the girdles worn for service in the tabernacle. There were two. They were to hold the other garments together. They are called waistbands in some versions of the Bible.

The girdle is a symbol of readiness. A girdle was worn by the general population when they wanted to go to work, to fight, or to serve their masters. They did not want their other garments to hinder their movement, so they tied them in the girdle, the waistband. On the night of the first Passover, the Hebrews were getting ready to leave Egypt by girding their loins, putting on their shoes, and taking up their staffs. Jesus's girdle was a symbol of His readiness to serve as when He girded Himself with a towel to wash His disciples' feet in John 13.

I think of tins of Heinz tomato soup, which used to have the words *ready to serve* on the label. In the nineteenth century, Henry John and Ann Heinz were committed Christians, and when they set up their business, they decided that the motto "ready to serve" epitomized their ambition. They were ready to serve Christ.

The high priest wore a plain girdle around the plain coat. The other outer garments of beauty were removed on the Day of Atonement when he went into the holy of holies. This spoke of the service Jesus performed on earth two thousand years ago.

Earthly Service

In Mark 10:45, we read that Jesus said, "I am not come to be served, but to serve, and to give My life a ransom for many." This speaks of the humility and humanity of Christ, who laid aside His glory and took the form of a man to go to Calvary.

The high priest dressed in the plain coat with a plain girdle on the Day of Atonement was an illustration of Jesus's readiness to present Himself as the sacrifice for our sins on Calvary's cross.

The second girdle worn by the high priest was the beautifully embroidered one worn over the robe of the ephod. This was worn on all other occasions by the high priest when he carried out his office of representing the people before God.

Heavenly Service

So, the description of the high priest in Old Testament times is a picture of the Lord Jesus as our great High Priest able to represent all believers in the presence of God, in His present and ongoing intercession for us, with our names on His shoulders for security and strength, and our names also on his breast assuring us that we are loved and that nothing can separate us from His love. We read in Hebrews 8:1–2 (ESV),

> Now the point in what we are saying is this; we have such a high priest, one who is seated at the right hand of the throne of the Majesty in heaven, a minister in the holy places, in the true tent that the Lord set up, not man.

In Hebrews 7:24–25 (NIV), we read,

> Because Jesus lives forever, He has a permanent priesthood. Therefore, He is able to save completely those who come to God through Him, because He always lives to intercede for them.

Then in Revelation 1:12–16, we read of John's vision of the Son of Man girded about the breast with a golden girdle. This is the Lord Jesus Christ in His judicial capacity in a future day, His eyes as a flame of fire and describing Himself as the First and Last. Gold indicates His deity. And His girdle is described in Isaiah 11:5 as faithfulness and righteousness: "And righteousness shall be the girdle of his loins, and faithfulness the girdle of his reins."

Our Girdle

We too have girdles; 1 Peter 1:13 reads, "Wherefore, gird up the loins of your mind."

> Let your loins be girded about, and your lights burning; and ye yourselves like unto men that wait for their lord, when he will return from the wedding; that when he cometh and knocketh, they may open unto him immediately. Blessed are those servants, whom the lord when he cometh shall find watching; verily I say unto you, that he shall gird himself, and make them to sit down to meat, and will come forth and serve them. (Luke 12:35–37)

Debt

13

The UK and the US are debt-ridden. They have overspent their budgets by trillions, not just billions, of pounds and dollars, and many other countries are debt-ridden too.

With the pandemic and unemployment, people are finding it hard to pay off their credit cards; that type of debt is over £1 trillion in the UK. As a result, homelessness is on the rise and foodbanks are on the increase.

What a dire situation. "If only we could settle all our debts" is the cry of the world. Iraq owes the US and Germany $64.5 billion, and it has been agreed to write it off. What a terrific burden a debt can be; like a stranglehold.

Do you ever think that we are indebted to God, our Maker?

In Luke 16, we have a parable of the manager of the estate of a rich man; he had allowed the debtors to get out of control, and he had to do something quickly to recover the debt lest he be sacked for incompetence. So, he went to each debtor and asked, "How much do you owe my master?" (Luke 16:5–6 NASU).

Can we ask ourselves the same question about the debt we owe God? Think of His grace in giving us freely what we do not deserve and withholding the judgment we deserve and settling a debt we could not pay.

The psalmist asked in Psalm 116:12 (NLT), "What shall I give to the Lord in return for all His benefits?" The truth is that we are poverty-stricken. We have nothing we can give God. In fact, the psalmist gave a strange answer. "Not I will give, but I will take. I will take the cup of salvation."

When we think of all He has done for us, the only proper response should be to give ourselves to Him and take the salvation He offers.

In Matthew 22:21 (RSV), we read,

> Jesus said to the pharisees in answer to their question whether it was right to pay taxes to Caesar, show me a coin. Whose image is on the coin? Caesar's, they replied. Jesus said, then render unto Caesar that which is Caesar's and unto God that which is God's.

The image of God is on humankind.

The greatest of God's blessings is forgiveness of sin. I love the words of a hymn we sometimes sing: "Jesus paid it all; all to Him I owe." We could not pay for it ourselves.

In Psalm 103, David realized how gracious the Lord was: "Bless the Lord, O my soul, and forget not all His benefits: Who forgives all your iniquities."

In the past, forgiving a debt meant cancelling it; the meaning of the Greek word is cancel, send away, or dismiss. In those days, if a Jew was unable to pay a debt, he would pin the unpaid bill to his front door hoping that some generous benefactor would come along, see the bill, pay it, and nail the paid bill to the door with the word *tetelestai* written across it. The word *tetelestai* was also written on business documents or receipts in New Testament times to indicate that a bill had been paid in full. When Jesus cried on the cross, He said, "Tetelestai." He was saying in effect "It is finished … It is paid"; He had paid the penalty for our sins in full. Paul wrote that Jesus took the list of sins recorded against us and nailed it to His cross taking them away.

When He forgives our sins, He remembers them no more. I remember a story told by my Bible class teacher Cliff Beer, when we were teenagers in North Clive Street Gospel Hall youth class in Cardiff. It is the story of an office boy who was given the responsibility of looking after the petty cash box. Sadly, the boy fell to temptation and stole some money from the box. When the shortage was discovered, the boy was brought before his boss. He admitted what he had done, and graciously, the boss said to him, "I forgive you this time, but don't let it happen again." However, every time they passed each other in the corridor, they both remembered what had happened, and the boy felt guilty whenever he saw his boss.

Not so with the Lord Jesus. I cannot say He forgives and forgets because God does not forget, but in a positive way, He remembers no more. Not like John F. Kennedy, who said, "Forgive your enemies, but never forget their names."

Jesus told His disciples who found it hard to forgive, to be generous in forgiving. He told a parable of a king who had a servant who owed him ten thousand talents.

> The kingdom of heaven may be compared to a king who wished to settle accounts with his servants. When he began to settle, one was brought to him who owed him ten thousand talents. And since he could not pay, his master ordered him to be sold, with his wife and children and all that he had, and payment to be made. So, the servant fell on his knees, imploring him, "Have patience with me, and I will pay you everything." And out of pity for

him, the master of that servant released him and forgave him the debt.

But when that same servant went out, he found one of his fellow servants who owed him a hundred denarii, and seizing him, he began to choke him, saying, "Pay what you owe." So, his fellow servant fell down and pleaded with him, "Have patience with me, and I will pay you." He refused and went and put him in prison until he should pay the debt.

When his fellow servants saw what had taken place, they were greatly distressed, and they went and reported to their master all that had taken place. Then his master summoned him and said to him, "You wicked servant! I forgave you all that debt because you pleaded with me. And should not you have had mercy on your fellow servant, as I had mercy on you?" And in anger his master delivered him to the jailers, until he should pay all his debt. So also, my heavenly Father will do to every one of you, if you do not forgive your brother from your heart. (Matthew 18:23–35 ESV)

This is a reminder of the debt we owed God that Jesus settled at Calvary. In the prayer the Lord taught His disciples, He taught them to pray, "And forgive us our debts, as we forgive our debtors" (Matthew 6:12).

14

Metamorphosis

The word *metamorphosis* reminds me of the way God miraculously changes the nature of the Christian. Who would imagine that an ugly caterpillar could change into a beautiful butterfly? How can a wretched, sinful person like you or me gain a new nature? How can the fallen nature of humankind be changed into something beautiful?

We find the answer in the Bible: "If any man be in Christ, he is a new creature: old things are passed away; behold, all things are become new." A modern translation reads, "When someone becomes a Christian, he becomes a brand-new person inside. He is not the same anymore. A new life has begun!" (2 Corinthians 5:17 TLB).

We read in John 3 that Jesus said to Nicodemus, "You must be born again." If you want a metamorphosis, a new nature, you must have a new birth. Jesus said,

> No one can enter the Kingdom of God without being born of water and the Spirit. Humans can reproduce only human life, but the Holy Spirit gives birth to spiritual life. So don't be surprised

when I say, You must be born again. (John
3:5-7(NLT).

Nicodemus asked, "How can a man be born again?" The
answer was in the verse we first read: "If any man be in Christ,
he is a new creature."

The Process of Metamorphosis

When my brother and I were young, we were interested in
insects of all kinds. We would watch ants carrying their food
to their storehouse marching in columns just like soldiers. We
would watch spiders catching flies in their beautiful silk webs.
How interesting it was to study centipedes with their many
legs, sometimes more than one hundred, not to mention the
woodlouse, which would curl up into an armor-coated ball if
touched.

All this intrigued me then, but when I attended high school,
the subject of biology did not impress me at all. But I remember my
interest in insects and amphibians that underwent metamorphoses
and in particular caterpillars and tadpoles.

When we were boys, we would go to an area we called the
droves, which had ponds and reeds and plenty of wildlife. It was a
natural habitat for dragonflies, butterflies, grasshoppers, tadpoles,
and frogs. We would catch tadpoles and put them in jam jars, take
them home, and watch them develop one leg at a time and turn
into frogs. I would have said that the ugly tadpoles turned into
ugly frogs but that the ugly caterpillars developed into beautiful
butterflies.

Think of the lifestyle of a caterpillar. How boring! Basically,
all it does is feed on leaves in preparation for the next stage in its
development, which is to become a chrysalis. *Surely there must
be more to life than this*, it must think. *I may as well be a cow*

eating grass all my life and never seeing the beautiful mountains and forests. How boring! It does not realize that a day would come when its life will change for the better. It is the plan of God, its Creator, that an ugly caterpillar should become a beautiful butterfly.

Once the chrysalis sheds its outer skin, it reveals beautiful wings. We use the phrase "to spread your wings" to mean to discover your potential, to move into new territory. This is sometimes a picture of you and me as believers in the Lord Jesus. Before we became followers of the Lord, we were ugly caterpillars, sinners. But after we were saved, our lives were transformed. It is as if we too had developed wings we could spread, and accomplish some of the things God had planned for us. Sadly, we sometimes fail to recognize that we are no longer caterpillars and cling to our past lives and old habits. It takes some time to accept and discover what our wings are for.

When we trusted the Lord Jesus, we were made anew; we became new creations with new natures. How wonderful when we think that in Jesus Christ we have been transformed and that it is God's plan for us to keep changing until we reach the likeness of His Son.

In Romans 12:2 we read, "And be not conformed to this world: but be ye transformed by the renewing of your mind, that ye may prove what is that good, and acceptable, and perfect, will of God."

In Romans 8:29, Paul wrote that we were to be conformed to the image of the Lord Jesus: "For whom he did foreknow, he also did predestinate to be conformed to the image of his Son." To become like Christ is our goal.

In Philippians 3:20–21 (NLT), Paul wrote,

> He will take our weak mortal bodies and change them into glorious bodies like his own and

using the same power with which he will bring everything under his control.

And in 2 Corinthians 3:18 (NIV), Paul wrote,

> And we all, who with unveiled faces contemplate the Lord's glory, are being transformed into his image with ever-increasing glory, which comes from the Lord, who is the Spirit.

After being reborn, we can mature into our identities as God's sons and daughters by feeding on His Word just as butterflies feed on nectar. Psalm 119:103 reads, "How sweet are thy words unto my taste! yea, sweeter than honey to my mouth!"

Referring to one's ambition to mature and grow more like Christ, Paul wrote in Ephesians 4:11–16 (NLT),

> Now these are the gifts Christ gave to the church: the apostles, the prophets, the evangelists, and the pastors and teachers. Their responsibility is to equip God's people to do his work and build up the church, the body of Christ. This will continue until we all come to such unity in our faith and knowledge of God's Son that we will be mature in the Lord, measuring up to the full and complete standard of Christ.
>
> Then we will no longer be immature like children. We won't be tossed and blown about by every wind of new teaching. We will not be influenced when people try to trick us with lies so clever, they sound like the truth. Instead, we will speak the truth in love, growing in every way more and more like Christ, who is the head of his body, the

church. He makes the whole body fit together perfectly. As each part does its own special work, it helps the other parts grow, so that the whole body is healthy and growing and full of love.

Praise God! He is changing me.

Seeds

15

What do apples, oranges, nuts, corn, dates, and dandelions have in common? Yes—seeds. Some seeds estimated to be thousands of years old are still capable of growing into plants. A date palm was given the name of Methuselah because the seed from which it grew was estimated to be two thousand years old. It was planted less than twenty years after it was discovered in 1963 during an excavation of Herod the Great's fortress of Masada near the Dead Sea.

The biggest seed, legendary because of its size, belongs to the coco de mer palm tree. Its fruit usually contains just one seed, but it can weigh several stones. They grow only on two islands in the Seychelles.

You may have found some wonderful tasting apples, but if you plant its seed, it will grow into an apple with a taste completely different from the one you originally ate. For example, a seed from a Golden Delicious or a Granny Smith apple will not grow into an apple with the same looks and taste. Each apple seed will produce offspring that are individual and quite unlike their parents. Humans share this tendency but to a much lesser extent.

I have a Christian friend who is from Kazakhstan, a former

Russian satellite country. I learned that Almaty, Kazakhstan's main city, means "Father of apples." It seems that the travelers on the great silk routes that crossed central Asia developed a taste for apples and spat their pips out wherever they rested. And now, apples are the most popular fruit in the world grown or traded on every continent. Someone has commented that "Any fool can count the seeds in an apple. Only God can count all the apples in one seed."

Did you know that bananas are seedless? They are propagated by a sucker off an existing plant. And did you know that one dandelion flower head produces two hundred seeds 99 percent of which travel less than ten meters in a breeze.

As you know, Jesus often took the familiar things people could relate to in order to explain spiritual or heavenly truths. He spoke of sheep and sheepfolds, vineyards, builders, and wedding feasts. Sometimes, He used parables and other times metaphors or similes to give ordinary things spiritual meaning.

This was the case when only a few days before He was to be crucified, Jesus told His disciples, "The hour is come, that the Son of man should be glorified. Except a corn of wheat fall into the ground and die, it abideth alone: but if it die, it bringeth forth much fruit" (John 12:23–24). He was speaking of His death on the cross. He likened Himself to a seed, a grain of wheat that went into the ground and died; only then could it produce fruit, indicating that many lost souls would be saved because of His death. He rose from the grave the triumphant Savior. The wonder of Calvary was that it brought forth much fruit. Many sinners were saved by Jesus's sacrifice and became children of God.

Hebrews 2:9–10 (NLT) reads,

> What we do see is Jesus, who was given a position a little lower than the angels; and because he suffered death for us, he is now crowned with glory and honour. Yes, by God's grace Jesus tasted

73

death for everyone. God, for whom and through whom everything was made, chose to bring many children into glory. And it was only right that he should make Jesus, through his suffering, a perfect leader, fit to bring them into their salvation.

Revelation 7:9–10 (NIV) reads,

> After this I looked and there before me was a great multitude that no one could count, from every tribe, nation, people, and language, standing before the throne and in front of the Lamb. They were wearing white robes and were holding palm branches in their hands. And they cried out in a loud voice: Salvation belongs to our God, who sits on the throne, and to the Lamb.

Grass seed left on the shelf will not grow; it must be planted. Jesus as a seed had to fall to the ground to produce much fruit.

In 1 Corinthians 15:42–44, Paul described the resurrection of a believer like a seed sown in the ground.

> So also is the resurrection of the dead. It is sown in corruption [decay]; it is raised in incorruption: it is sown in dishonour; it is raised in glory: it is sown in weakness; it is raised in power: it is sown a natural body; it is raised a spiritual body. There is a natural body, and there is a spiritual body.

Choices

16

We are different from all other animals in that we have ability to make choices; we have consciences, which help us distinguish between right and wrong; we have minds that enable us to reason between right and wrong; and we have free will to choose what is right or what is wrong. In Psalm 139:14, we read, "I will praise thee; for I am fearfully and wonderfully made: marvelous are thy works; that my soul knoweth right well."

We probably make hundreds of choices every day, some of which are easy while others are difficult; some are trivial while others are important. Some have little effect on our lives while others can have serious consequences.

Not long ago, India, as a developing nation, decided to introduce pesticides and other toxic chemicals into its farming practices to improve harvests to feed the growing population; it was called the Green Revolution. But they soon found that the incidence of cancer greatly increased as did birth defects, stillborn babies, and other life-threatening diseases. They made the wrong choice, and it had disastrous consequences.

We have recently been witnessing the outcome of the election of a new US president, and the result of the people's choice

75

will probably have far-reaching consequences for the country's populace.

The Bible is full of people whose choices affected their lives and their nations. Adam and Eve chose to disobey God, and the result was that humankind inherited from them a sinful nature. That was about the most tragic choice ever made.

Abraham made a choice when he took Hagar, Sarah's handmaid, resulting in the birth of Ishmael. He was impatient for God to fulfill His promise of an heir, and that led to tragic consequences and conflict throughout the ages between Jews and Arabs.

Read Genesis 13, in which Abram and his nephew Lot made some choices. God had told Abram to leave his home in Ur, and he obeyed God. We find him, at age seventy-five, and Lot making their way to Canaan, the land God had promised to Abram and his issue.

However, there was a famine in the land, and the group made their way to Egypt, where there was plenty of food. But this was probably a wrong step by Abram, out of line with God's will, because we find that Abram, to save his own skin, passed off his wife Sarah, as his sister. It was only through the leniency of Pharaoh that Abram's life was spared, and they were sent packing out of Egypt. Talking about choice. That was obviously the wrong choice Abram made by going down into Egypt.

They made their way north back to Bethel, where Abram had first built an altar to the Lord. There, Abram sought God's forgiveness and made a new commitment to go only where God would lead him. The Bible does not tell us this, but it says "And there Abram called on the Name of the Lord." (Gen 13:4).

We read that there was strife among the herdsmen of Lot and Abram, who by then had many cattle. The Bible says that Abram was very rich in cattle, silver, and gold and that Lot also had many herds and flocks and tents. The land could not support them all, so rather than prolong the unpleasantness and strife, Abram decided it would be best if they split up and went their separate ways. At that point, choices were made. Abram trusted God to lead him in the right direction. This is how believers should commit to the Lord, not go their own way.

We read that Lot saw the well-watered plain of Jordan, where he then went. He pitched his tent near the wicked city of Sodom and then took up residence in it. Finally, we find him as a member of the city council. Sodom was such a wicked city as was Gomorrah, a nearby city, that God later destroyed them with fire and brimstone. It was only through the intercession of Abram that Lot was saved.

What led Lot to make the choice he made? The Bible says, "Lot lifted up his eyes"; he was influenced by what he saw. The Bible calls it "the lust of the eyes" (1 John 2:16). Proverbs 27:20 states, "The eyes of man are never satisfied."

Lot must have been influenced by the superficial. He saw only lush, well-watered plains, not the evil in the cities just over the horizon. He chose the broad road seeking pleasure, material things, and prosperity.

In Matthew 6, Jesus said,

> Lay not up for yourselves treasures upon the earth where moth and rust doth corrupt and where thieves break through and steal but lay up for yourselves treasures in heaven … you cannot serve God and mammon [the idol of riches].

On the other hand, Abram chose God's way (Hebrews 11:10): "By faith Abram looked for a city which hath foundations, whose builder and maker is God." He did what we all should do and as Jesus told us: "Seek ye first the Kingdom of God." We should not be influenced by the superficial, the outward appearance of things. We are reminded in scripture that God looks on the heart, not the outward appearance.

When Jesus was brought before Pilate on trumped-up charges, he realized that Jesus had done nothing wrong. He knew Barabbas was a murderer, a robber, and a terrorist, so Pilate thought that if he gave the masses the choice of whom he should release, they would surely choose Jesus.

> "Who shall I release, Barabbas or Jesus who is called the Christ?" But the unanimous response came from the crowd, "Barabbas, release Barabbas and crucify Jesus!" (Matthew 27:17–21)

And so innocent Jesus was crucified. It so happened that it was all in God's plan that Jesus should die on the cross so that He might bear the penalty for our sin.

The apostle Paul said, "For to me to live is Christ, and to die is gain" (Philippians 1:21).

I thank the Lord that I made the right choice when I said, "Christ for me!"

Godliness

17

Reading: Romans 8:29

> For whom He did foreknow, He also did predestinate
> to be conformed to the image of his Son.

To be like Jesus is to walk like Him (1 John 2:6), love like Him (John 13:34), think like Him (Philippians 2:5), act like Him (John 13:15), and be holy like Him (1 Peter 1:15).

In the pastoral epistles, several themes seem to be emphasized including sound doctrine and godliness. The word *godliness* occurs fifteen times in the New Testament; fourteen of them are in the pastoral epistles, and eight of those are in 1 Timothy. Look out for this word in these readings.

> I exhort therefore, that, first of all, supplications, prayers, intercessions, and giving of thanks be made for all men; for kings, and for all that are in authority; that we may lead a quiet and peaceable life in all godliness and honesty. For this is good

and acceptable in the sight of God our Saviour. (1 Timothy 2:1–3)

And without controversy great is the mystery of godliness: God was manifest in the flesh, justified in the Spirit, seen of angels, preached unto the Gentiles, believed on in the world, received up into glory. (1 Timothy 3:16)

If any man teach otherwise, and consent not to wholesome words, even the words of our Lord Jesus Christ, and to the doctrine which is according to godliness; he is proud, knowing nothing, but doting about questions and strifes of words, whereof cometh envy, strife, railings, evil surmisings, perverse disputings of men of corrupt minds, and destitute of the truth, supposing that gain is godliness: from such withdraw thyself.

But godliness with contentment is great gain. For we brought nothing into this world, and it is certain we can carry nothing out. And having food and raiment let us be therewith content.

But thou, O man of God, flee these things; and follow after righteousness, godliness, faith, love, patience, meekness. (1 Timothy 6:3–11)

It is not surprising when you consider that Paul addressed Timothy as a "man of God" that the subject of godliness should be prominent in his letters to Timothy.

Psalm 1 describes the man of God (the godly man) as a very happy man and then describes his activities whether walking, sitting, or standing.

Blessed is the man who walks not in the counsel of
the ungodly, nor stands in the path of sinners, nor
sits in the seat of the scornful; but his delight is in
the law of the Lord, and in His law he meditates
day and night. (Psalm 1:1–2 NKJV)

The Greek word for "godliness" is *eusebia*, which means "very
devout." Believers are devoutly consecrated and dedicated to God.
In the Old Testament, Ruth was a very good example of one
who showed devotion to a person, Naomi. In Ruth 1:16–17, we
read,

And Ruth said, Intreat me not to leave thee, or
to return from following after thee; for whither
thou goest I will go; and where thou lodgest, I will
lodge; thy people shall be my people, and thy God
my God; where thou diest, will I die, and there
will I be buried: the Lord do so to me, and more
also, if ought but death part thee and me.

We speak of some believers as godly men and women, those
who display godliness in their lives. Jesus is the perfect example
of godliness. In 1 Timothy 3:16, we read "Without controversy
great is the mystery of Godliness." What was once a mystery was
revealed—God was manifested in the flesh. Jesus took on the
likeness of men (Philippians 2:7) and displayed complete devotion
and consecration to His Father while on earth. He is the very
essence of God. Our ambition should be to be more like Christ,
but the true likeness will happen only when we are in heaven. In
1 John 3:2, we read, "But we know that, when He shall appear,
we shall be like Him; for we shall see him as He is."

In 1 Timothy 6:11–12, Paul wrote, "But thou, O man of God,
flee these things; and follow after righteousness, godliness, faith,
love, patience, meekness. Fight the good fight of faith."

These three make it easy to remember: flee, follow, fight. The verbs are in the present continuous tense; we are to keep on fleeing, following, and fighting.

"Flee these things." What are we to flee from? Paul had been telling Timothy in 1 Timothy 6:6–11 that godliness with contentment was great gain. We should be content with what God has provided us. We have food and clothing; let us be content therewith. Otherwise, we will be caught in the trap of worldliness of wanting and never being satisfied.

Paul described the trap as "many foolish and harmful desires" (NLT) that plunged them into ruin and destruction "For the love of money is the root of all kinds of evil. And some people, craving money, have wandered from the true faith, and pierced themselves with many sorrows." (1 Timothy 6:10 (NLT).

These things are our enemies chasing us and ready to strike. Paul said that the man or woman of God should flee from these things and not entertain them. Our consciences tell us that they are wrong as does the Word, so we are not to dabble in them lest we become addicted to them like drugs.

Paul wrote that we were to "follow after righteousness, godliness, faith, love, patience and meekness." Did you notice that godliness is one of the virtues we should follow?

Paul reminded Timothy of the Christian's fight in 2 Timothy 2:3–4 (TLB); as "Christ's soldier, do not let yourself become tied up in worldly affairs, for then you cannot satisfy the one who has enlisted you in his army."

When Paul was nearing the end of his life on earth, he could say with confidence, "I have fought a good fight, I have finished my course, I have kept the faith" (2 Timothy 4:7).

In 2 Peter 3:11, we read, "Seeing then that all these things shall be dissolved, what manner of persons ought ye to be in all holy manner of life and godliness."

Joshua 24:15–18 (NKJV) reads,

Choose for yourselves this day whom you will serve, whether the gods which your fathers served that were on the other side of the river, or the gods of the Amorites, in whose land you dwell. But as for me and my house, we will serve the Lord. So the people answered and said: Far be it from us that we should forsake the Lord to serve other gods; for the Lord our God is He who brought us and our fathers up out of the land of Egypt, from the house of bondage, who did those great signs in our sight, and preserved us in all the way that we went and among all the people through whom we passed. And the Lord drove out from before us all the people, including the Amorites who dwelt in the land. We also will serve the Lord, for He is our God.

18

The Threshing Floor

Threshing floors were important places in Middle Eastern countries during biblical times since farming was their main source of food. These floors were specially prepared usually in fields on flat rocks open to the wind and therefore usually elevated.

These were places where wheat and barley crops were threshed usually with flails, long staffs, or sledges drawn by oxen or horses. After the harvest had been threshed, it was sieved and fanned so that the chaff would be blown away leaving the grain.

The Bible often uses the figure of the threshing floor to represent a crisis point in the lives of individuals and nations alike. Sometimes, the threshing floor was used to represent the separation by God of the lost souls from the saved. In Hosea 13:3, the idolatrous nation was described by the prophet as "the chaff that is driven with the whirlwind out of the floor." And in Job 21:18, the wicked were described as "chaff that the storm carrieth away."

The threshing floor would have been a very important place in any town or village, a strategic place where vital decisions were made. On several occasions in scripture, it was the place where an angel confronted men for whom God had special messages at times of crises and times when God issued challenges. Sometimes, it was the place where an altar to God was built to mark the fact that God had been there and where sacrifices to God were made. We read of the threshing floor of Atad in Genesis 50:1–21.

Crisis in the Family

It was a time of crisis for Joseph because his father, Jacob, had died. His father had brought him up for seventeen years, and then for the last seventeen years of Jacob's life, Joseph cared for his father in his old age in Egypt. This must have been a happy period for the two after having been apart for so long. Joseph had promised his father that he would bury him in the land of his fathers, Canaan, not in Egypt.

The funeral cortege, which consisted of many Egyptian servants and nobles as well as Joseph's brothers, made its way to Canaan with the body of Jacob, which they had embalmed. They stopped at the threshing floor at Atad and stayed for seven days mourning. The Bible says it was a "great and very sore lament." So this threshing floor was a place of mourning.

In Judges 9:14–15, the name Atad is rendered as "brambles," and in Psalm 58:9, it is "thorns." It was quite a prickly and critical time in Joseph's life. We all must come to this threshing floor at some time or another including when we lose loved ones. Ecclesiastes 3:4 tells us that there is "a time to weep, and a time to laugh; a time to mourn."

How do we cope? In Matthew 5:4, Jesus said, "Blessed are they that mourn: for they shall be comforted."

In 2 Corinthians 1:3–5 (NLT). Paul wrote,

> All praise to God, the Father of our Lord Jesus Christ. God is our merciful Father and the source of all comfort. He comforts us in all our troubles

so that we can comfort others. When they are troubled, we will be able to give them the same comfort God has given us. For the more we suffer for Christ, the more God will shower us with His comfort through Christ.

And if your loved one is a believer, Paul wrote in 1 Thessalonians 4:13–14,

> But I would not have you to be ignorant, brethren, concerning them which are asleep, that ye sorrow not, even as others which have no hope. For if we believe that Jesus died and rose again, even so them also which sleep in Jesus will God bring with him.

Joseph's Brothers

It was also a time of crisis for Joseph's brothers because they thought that now that their father was dead, Joseph would take his revenge on them for their cruelty to him in earlier days. Their consciences were still troubling them though Joseph had forgiven them seventeen years earlier when they had first come to Egypt for corn when he revealed himself to them as we read in Genesis 45:2–5, when Joseph told them,

> Come near to me, I pray you. And they came near. And he said, I am Joseph your brother, whom ye sold into Egypt. Now therefore be not grieved, nor angry with yourselves, that ye sold me hither: for God did send me before you to preserve life; I will nourish you.

Joseph had forgiven them, but they had not been living in the blessing and assurance of it. Could it be that they had never repented? We do not read of any repentance on their part. But now they realized what danger they could be in, and they confessed their sin, and so they repented and asked Joseph to forgive them again. He responded generously weeping as he forgave them once again and comforted them. It was a case of déjà vu—they had been there before. He said, "You thought evil against me, but God meant it for good." Joseph repeated what he had told them those many years earlier: "I will nourish you."

Are we living in the conscious knowledge and blessing of knowing that God has forgiven our sins, or are our consciences not settled? Are we thinking of sins that Christ has already forgiven maybe years ago? In 1 John 1:9, we read, "If we confess our sins, He is faithful and just to forgive us our sins and to cleanse us from all unrighteousness."

Joseph's example teaches us another lesson—We should forgive one another even as Christ taught us to forgive one another. Paul wrote about this in Ephesians 4:30–32.

> And grieve not the holy Spirit of God, whereby ye are sealed unto the day of redemption. Let all bitterness, and wrath, and anger, and clamour, and evil speaking, be put away from you, with all malice: And be ye kind one to another, tender hearted, forgiving one another, even as God for Christ's sake hath forgiven you.

Christ's cross could be regarded as a threshing floor because it was also a place where a crisis was enacted. Indeed, some believe the cross was erected on the same site as the threshing floor of Ornan on Mount Moriah, where Abraham offered his son, Isaac, as a burnt offering to the Lord and where Isaac was spared. In 1 Chronicles 21:20–22, we read,

> And as David came to Ornan, Ornan looked and
> saw David, and went out of the threshing floor,
> and bowed himself to David with his face to the
> ground. Then David said to Ornan, Grant me the
> place of this threshing floor, that I may build an
> altar therein unto the Lord.

In Hebrews 9:26, reference is made to "the end of the world." This really means "the climax of the ages," when Christ died on the cross. And again, in John 12:31, Jesus referred to His death on the cross as "the judgement of this world." This phrase means in Greek "the crisis of this world" where "crisis" means a separation, a time of decision.

How apt that the purpose of a threshing floor was to separate the chaff from the wheat. John the Baptist described Jesus in Matthew 3:12 as the one who separated the wheat from the chaff: "Whose fan is in his hand, and he will throughly purge his floor, and gather his wheat into the garner; but he will burn up the chaff with unquenchable fire."

Have you been to the threshing floor?

19

King George VI

A few years ago, the movie *The King's Speech* came out and was nominated for an Oscar. It was about how King George VI overcame his stammering.

Some things that happen to us make such indelible marks on our memories that we remember where we were when the news of these events took place. For example, the assassination of President Kennedy, the tragic death of Princess Diana, and the Twin Towers disaster.

I can remember exactly where I was when the news of the death of King George VI was announced in 1952. I was in school, and all the children were called into the assembly hall, where the headmaster announced the passing of the king.

I believe George VI trusted in the Lord Jesus, and when he gave his Christmas broadcast in December 1939, as Britain was facing World War II, he quoted from a poem by Louise Haskins, indicating that he was trusting God by placing his hand into the safe hand of God and walking into an unknown future. He encouraged the British people to do the same as they were facing war.

It is said that before the abdication of his brother, Edward VIII, he used to attend Bible readings at a church in London.

It is recorded that on a state visit to Canada in 1937, King George was introduced to White Feather, a famous Indian chief. White Feather was a true believer in the Lord Jesus and a famous baritone singer. The Indian chief announced that he would like to sing a song to King George. Everyone expected a tribal song, but the chief sang a hymn that later became the favorite song of George Beverley Shea. It was entitled "I'd Rather Have Jesus Than Silver or Gold." The officials were stunned when King George responded by saying, "I too, would rather have Jesus."

The whole country loved King George VI because with humility and dedication, he accepted the role of sovereign. They loved him because he identified with the people of London during the blitz, and even though Buckingham Palace had been hit, the royal family stayed in London.

He must have loved to read the Bible; this was the message from His Majesty inscribed in New Testaments given to all British forces in World War II.

> To all serving in my forces by sea or land, or in the air, and indeed, to all my people engaged in the defence of the Realm, I commend the reading of this book. For centuries the Bible has been a wholesome and strengthening influence in our national life, and it behoves us in these momentous days to turn with renewed faith to this divine source of comfort and inspiration.

King George VI was not born to be a king and had not been groomed or prepared for it, but he took on the responsibility bravely despite his stuttering. This recalls the fact that when Jesus was born, He was not born to be king because He was already a king. The wise men asked the question, "Where is He that is born King of the Jews?" (Matthew 2:2).

Again, at His mock trial, Jesus was explicit in his reply to Pilate. In John 18:37 (NKJV), we read,

> Pilate therefore said to Him, Are You a king then? Jesus answered, "you say rightly that I am a king. For this cause I was born, and for this cause I have come into the world, that I should bear witness to the truth. Everyone who is of the truth hears My voice.

The Bible records the story of David, the greatest king of Israel, who like George VI had not been born to be a king. Indeed, just like Jesus, he was born in the little town of Bethlehem and had probably grown up largely unnoticed. He was just a shepherd boy, the youngest son of Jesse, and in the eyes of King Saul, he was of no consequence when it came to fighting the enemy of Israel.

However, because of David's keenness to defeat Goliath, he convinced King Saul of his prowess in being able to protect his sheep by killing a lion and a bear and even more significantly showing to Saul that the Lord would deliver him out of the hand of the enemy. The king gave David permission to fight Goliath. This is all recorded in 1 Samuel 17:32–37.

> And David said to Saul, let no man's heart fail because of him; thy servant will go and fight with this Philistine. And Saul said to David, thou art not able to go against this Philistine to fight with him, for thou art but a youth, and he a man of war from his youth. And David said unto Saul, thy servant kept his father's sheep, and there came a lion, and a bear, and took a lamb out of the flock: Thy servant slew both the lion and the bear: and

this uncircumcised Philistine shall be as one of them, seeing he hath defied the armies of the living God. David said moreover, The Lord that delivered me out of the paw of the lion, and out of the paw of the bear, he will deliver me out of the hand of this Philistine. And Saul said unto David, Go, and the Lord be with thee.

Even higher praise came from God through the speech of Stephen in Acts. Stephen quoted the Lord as saying, "I have found David the son of Jesse a man after my own heart. Of this man's seed hath God according to his promise raised unto Israel a Saviour, Jesus" (Acts 13:22–23).

In 1 Timothy 6:15, Paul declared Jesus as King of Kings at His appearing to reign "which in His times He shall show, who is the blessed and only Potentate, the King of kings, and Lord of lords."

Who is reigning in your life? Is He a dethroned King, or is He sitting on the throne of your heart?

20

The Lame Man

Reading: Acts 3:1–16

There are at least six reasons Jesus healed the sick man in this reading.

1. It expressed the mind and will of God.
2. It was a sign of His compassion.
3. It fulfilled prophecy.
4. It brought wholeness.
5. God was glorified in it.
6. It stimulated faith in the disciples.

Luke 9:1–2 reads, "Then he called his twelve disciples together, and gave them power and authority over all devils, and to cure diseases, and he sent them to preach the kingdom of God, and to heal the sick."

The following features characterized Peter and John.

They were staunch companions. Though they were opposites in character, they worked successfully together. John was the disciple who spoke often of love in his letters; he was gentle, whereas Peter was an impetuous man full of action who made many mistakes. We could say, "Whenever he opened his mouth, he put his foot in it."

They were spiritual. They were controlled by the Holy Spirit. They had not long experienced the filling of the Holy Spirit on the Day of Pentecost.

They were surrendered men. They were men of prayer. We know this because we read "They went up together into the temple at the hour of prayer." (Acts 3:1). They had been in the presence of God in the temple daily praising God.

They were sympathetic. As the lame man asked for help, the scripture tells us of Peter's and John's responses, saying "Look on us," in other words, "We can help you." Faith blended with prayer made them willing to help.

They were humble men. They had no money, nothing material. "Silver and gold have I none," said Peter. But they had resources of divine power.

They had the power and presence of God. They had spiritual assets. God can use men and women who have these qualities but are not necessarily intellectually clever or rich in this world's wealth.

In the incident of the lame man in Acts 3, I point out three important facts.

The **need** that confronted the disciples …

It was an extreme need. It was the need of a sad cripple (vv. 2–3). He could not work and provide for himself. He depended on others. Lame from birth, he had been carried by friends to the temple gate every day for forty years (4:22) and still no cure. No human could heal him. Doesn't this remind you of the great need of the world today where the disease of sin needs to be dealt with?

The need was expressed in verse 3, when the lame man asked for charity. In verse 5, we read that "he expected to receive something."

His interest was also encouraged by the disciples' response, "Look on us!" (v. 5), and so "He gave heed unto them."

Before we came to Christ, we were just like that lame man. Romans 5:6 reads, "For when we were yet without strength, in due time Christ died for the ungodly."

The **name** that cured the crippled man ...

In chapter 3 of our reading, Peter explained to the people that it was not by his or John's power that the lame man was healed. He explained to them in verse 16 (ESV),

> His name [the name of Jesus]—by faith in His name—has made this man strong whom you see and know, and the faith that is through Jesus has given the man this perfect health in the presence of you all.

The only name that could be called upon to heal this desperate man was Jesus's. Peter and John had no money, but Peter said, "What I do have, I give you. In the name of Jesus Christ of Nazareth, walk" (Acts 3:6 NIV).

Acts 4:12 reads, "Neither is there salvation in any other: for there is none other name under heaven given among men, whereby we must be saved."

Only through Jesus's name could this man be healed. The healing was decisive. It was immediate. It was divine. The man stood, walked, leaped; "All the people saw him," and it was a delightful healing; he entered the temple with them praising God (v. 8).

The startled crowd (vv. 10–16) ...

The crowd was amazed at divine power. "And they knew that it was he which sat for alms at the Beautiful gate of the temple: and they were filled with wonder and amazement at that which had happened unto him" (v. 10).

What did the rulers and elders recognize about Peter and John?

> Now when they saw the boldness of Peter and John, and perceived that they were unlearned and ignorant men, they marveled; and they took knowledge of them, that they had been with Jesus. (Acts 4:13)

Remember the two disciples who met Jesus after the resurrection on their way to Emmaus? They, too, had been with Jesus and their hearts burned as Jesus talked with them by the way (Luke 24:27–36).

> And beginning at Moses and all the prophets, he expounded unto them in all the scriptures the things concerning himself. And they drew nigh unto the village, whither they went, and he made as though he would have gone further. But they constrained him, saying, abide with us: for it is toward evening, and the day is far spent. And he went in to tarry with them. And it came to pass, as he sat at meat with them, he took bread, and blessed it, and brake, and gave to them.

And their eyes were opened, and they knew him; and he vanished out of their sight. And they said one to another, did not our heart burn within us, while he talked with us by the way, and while he opened to us the scriptures? And they rose up the same hour, and returned to Jerusalem, and found the eleven gathered together, and them that were with them, saying, The Lord is risen indeed, and hath appeared to Simon. And they told what things were done in the way, and how he was known of them in breaking of bread.

We should thank God that we treasure Jesus and His name.

Unto you therefore which believe he is precious
(1 Peter 2:7)

This is the subjective view of the Christian. But the word could also mean preciousness in the sense that whatever anyone else thinks of Jesus, He is intrinsically the preciousness.

God also hath highly exalted him and given him a name which is above every name: That at the name of Jesus every knee should bow, of things in heaven, and things in earth, and things under the earth; and that every tongue should confess that Jesus Christ is Lord, to the glory of God the Father. (Philippians 2:9–11)

The Beloved Disciple

21

The apostle John has been called the apostle of love. I counted his use of the word *love* in all its forms—well over a hundred times in his writings. Why do you imagine he was so sensitive to God's love? I believe it was because he was with Jesus as a disciple during those three years and witnessed so many wonderful things; he must have been convinced that the driving force in the life of Jesus was love—for His Father and all humankind no matter what their stations in life—rich or poor, young or old, good or bad, of high status or low.

In Mark 3:17, the Lord referred to John and his brother James as "Sons of Thunder," but John soon became known as "the disciple whom Jesus loved." Before I tell you what that means, I will say that it does not mean Jesus did not love the other disciples or that He loved John more than He loved the others. Jesus loves everyone.

In his gospel, John referred five times to the disciple whom Jesus loved without naming that disciple; it is John's way of referring to himself as the one Jesus loved. This is what is special about John; he knew he was loved by Jesus, and that gave him confidence and closeness to Christ. John must have been so thrilled that in effect he was saying, "Wow, Jesus loves even me!" The apostle Paul was also absorbed by the fact that God loved him. He wrote in Galatians 2:20 of "The Son of God who loved me and gave Himself for me."

> But let this great truth sink into our minds and hearts. Although God loves the world, and He loves the church, He continues to love you and me, even you, even me, with an everlasting love. This truth will motivate us as we strive to live our Christian lives.

Do we take God's love for granted and prefer to please ourselves rather than Him?

The disciple whom Jesus loved is referred to, as I said, five times in John's gospel. I am going to refer to two of these references.

The first reference suggests close communion. In the upper room when Jesus instituted the Lord's Table with the disciples, John recorded how Jesus was troubled in spirit and explained to His disciples that one of them would betray Him. John 13:22–27 reads,

> Then the disciples looked one on another, doubting of whom He spake. Now there was leaning on Jesus' bosom one of His disciples, whom Jesus loved. Simon Peter therefore beckoned to him, that he should ask who it should be of whom He spoke.
>
> He then lying on Jesus' breast saith unto Him, Lord, who is it? Jesus answered, He it is, to whom I shall give a sop, when I have dipped it. And when He had dipped the sop, He gave it to Judas

Iscariot, the son of Simon. And after the sop Satan
entered into him. Then said Jesus unto him, that
thou doest, do quickly.

Notice that Peter didn't ask Jesus who would betray Him, but
he asked John to ask Jesus. Obviously, Peter knew that John had a
close communion with the Savior, perhaps closer than he had, so
he asked John, and John asked Jesus, "Lord, who is it?" Jesus said
it was the one to whom He gave the sop after He has dipped it. It
was a confidence between Jesus and John.

The more we realize that God and Jesus love us, the more
our hearts will respond to His love and draw us closer to Him.
The more we appreciate His love for us, the more disposed we
will be to talk to Him in prayer and listen to His voice, to worship
and thank Him, and to read His Word. The closer we are to Him,
the more readily we will do His will, and by His grace, the more
likely He will place His confidence in us and entrust us with
responsibilities, commission us, and endow us with gifts to do His
will. How close are we to the Lord? Are we sometimes leaning on
His breast as it were?

Those who have pets can empathize when I say that some
of the outstanding examples of devotion and loyalty have been
displayed by our pets. There is a village in the Snowdonia region
of North Wales called Beddgelert with a population of fewer than
five hundred, but its name will go down in the folklore of Wales.
It is reputed to be named after the legendary hound Gelert. The
legend of Gelert goes back to the fifteenth century.

The story goes that in the thirteenth century, Prince Llewelyn
the Great had a palace in the area where the village is. He was a
keen hunter and had many hunting dogs. One day, he called all
his dogs with his horn to go hunting. But his favorite dog, Gelert,
did not appear, so the hunt went on without him.

When the hunt was over, the prince returned to his palace,
and Gelert came bounding toward him with blood dripping from

his mouth. The prince had the dreadful thought that Gelert had killed his one-year-old son, who had been sleeping in his cot in the nursery. When the prince ran into the nursery, he saw the cot upturned and blood spattered over the wall. He thought his worst fears had come true, and he drew his sword and lunged it into Gelert's heart. He then heard the weak cry of a child coming from the upturned cot. His baby was unharmed. And lying beside the child was a dead wolf. It dawned upon the prince that Gelert, his devoted and faithful dog, had saved his son from being killed by the wolf, and the prince was remorseful.

A grave of stones was erected where it is said Gelert was buried, and thousands of tourists visit it every year. That story whether true or only a legend illustrates in a very simple way what is true devotion to a master.

Years ago, there was a popular song. I remember the main theme was "To know him is to love him." This is so true of believers in the Lord Jesus, "To know Him is to love Him." Oh, that I would know Him more!

The second mention of the disciple whom Jesus loved is in John 21:4–8 and concerns spiritual sight.

> The disciples went fishing, but when the morning was come, they looked and saw a man on the shore. They could not tell who it was. When they brought in the fish, John writes that there was one who knew who it was! John, the disciple who Jesus loved, who said, "It is the Lord."

> But when the morning was now come, Jesus stood on the shore: but the disciples knew not that it was Jesus. Then Jesus saith unto them, Children, have ye any meat? They answered him, No. And He said unto them, Cast the net on the right side of the ship, and ye shall find.

They cast therefore, and now they were not able
to draw it for the multitude of fishes. Therefore,
that disciple whom Jesus loved saith unto Peter,
It is the Lord.

Only John recognized Jesus. I guess he had spiritual sight.
Sometimes, when we look around at our circumstances, we see
only what the world sees—the mundane, the carnal, the material,
things the Bible would refer to as things of the flesh, the cares of
this world. Others can see the hand of God in the things around
them even in times of sickness and need.

The disciple who is close to the Lord Jesus can see the hand of
God at work when others see only pain and grief. You can have a
deeper, fuller, and a closer relationship with God if you are willing
to sit near Him and listen to His voice.

22

A Balm in Gilead

The balm of Gilead is mentioned three times in the Bible. In Genesis 37:25 (NIV), we read, "They looked up and saw a caravan of Ishmaelites coming from Gilead. Their camels were loaded with spices, balm and myrrh."

When Jeremiah heard about how Babylon would besiege Israel, he wept and asked, "Is there no balm in Gilead? Is there no physician there?" (Jeremiah 8:22).

In Jeremiah 46:11, God told the Israelites to get a balm in Gilead because they had wounded themselves beyond repair.

We know that the balm of Gilead speaks of the Lord Jesus, the Great Physician.

Jeremiah wrote this warning to the nation of Judah of the impending invasion by the Assyrians and its consequent captivity in Babylon; he wrote that this was God's judgment on them for their backsliding and idolatry. They rejected his message and in effect sealed their fate. But Jeremiah was grief-stricken and cried out, "Is there no balm in Gilead? Is there no physician there?"

If many churches in the UK and in some other countries are not dying, they are showing signs of sickness and need the Lord's healing. Perhaps the Lord is telling us, "This sickness is not unto death, but for the glory of God" (John 11:4). The work of the Holy Spirit is to pour the balm of healing into our lives.

We rely on ointments and balms to heal our wounds, but there is a remedy that is free and for which there is no need to make an appointment with a doctor? It is the sun. Since before the time of ancient Egypt, doctors and natural healers relied on sunlight to repair wounds and treat bone diseases like rickets or lung infections like tuberculosis. Before antibiotics, sunlight was used to hasten the healing of wounds because sunlight is an efficient germ killer. As little as five to fifteen minutes of sunshine each day twice a week supplies enough vitamin D to keep one healthy.

The Bible describes Jesus as the sun of righteousness with healing powers. Malachi 4:2 reads, "But unto you that fear my name shall the Sun of righteousness arise with healing in his wings."

In 2 Chronicles 7:14 is another remedy for healing, this time for sin-sick souls. It was the prayer of King Solomon at the dedication of the temple he had built.

God's answer to King Solomon's prayer, which he prayed over four hundred years before Jeremiah's lamentations, gave the same remedy for the revival and for the healing of God's people through all the ages as well as today.

We ignore God and His Word at our peril. Because the children of Israel strayed from God, He allowed their enemies to conquer them, and they forfeited His blessing. Can you detect any parallel with our situation today? Are there many of the Lord's people still practicing idolatry in the sense that other things are taking the place of God?

Perhaps we can have a revival in our nation. We desperately need one. Revival starts with each one of us individually. God answered the prayer of King Solomon as we read in 2 Chronicles 7:14.

> If My people which are called by My name shall
> humble themselves, and pray and seek My face,
> and turn from their wicked ways, then will I hear
> from heaven, and will forgive their sin and will
> heal their land.

In this verse, we see the people who are the subject of this statement, the conditions for revival, and the promises obtained if the conditions are complied with. The verse is addressed to "my people." Yes, surely to the Israelites, but also to you and me. What a privilege to be called His people, we, who the Bible says were not a people but are now the people of God. We belong to Him; we read this in 1 Peter 2:9–10. We are God's possession bought with the precious blood of Christ. We are also called by His name. In Acts 15:14–17, Simeon said that the Lord had taken out of the Gentiles a people for His name.

> Simeon hath declared how God at the first did
> visit the Gentiles, to take out of them a people
> for his name. And to this agree the words of the
> prophets; as it is written, After this I will return,
> and will build again the tabernacle of David,
> which is fallen down; and I will build again the
> ruins thereof, and I will set it up: That the residue
> of men might seek after the Lord, and all the
> Gentiles, upon whom my name is called, saith
> the Lord, who doeth all these things.

Again, what a privilege and a responsibility; we must maintain a testimony that honors the Lord because we are called by His name. We should ask ourselves; do we honor His name in all we do? Are we ashamed of His name when we meet people?

Revival and healing are conditional. First, they require humility. God said, "If My people which are called by my name will humble themselves ..." In 1 Peter 5:5–6, we read, "God resisteth the proud, and giveth grace to the humble. Humble yourselves therefore under the mighty hand of God, that he may exalt you in due time."

We must get rid of our pride and humble ourselves before God. "Not I but Christ," said Paul. Psalm 8:4 reads, "What is man that thou art mindful of him?" When we pray to God, we should always remember that He is the God of the universe and that we are sinners though saved by grace.

I think pride is a besetting sin, one that seems to have a strong hold on me. In the days of the judges, it was said that the Jews did what was "right in their own eyes" (Judges 17:6). If it doesn't suit me, I don't want it. It should be not what I want but what God wants.

The second condition is that we must pray and seek His face if we want to receive His blessing. Seeking His face implies an intimacy, an earnestness in prayer, fervent, imploring and pleading, and asking for favor. We read in the Bible that His face may shine upon us, or He may turn His face from us.

The third condition for blessing is that we should turn from our wicked ways. What strong language. If we honestly examine our own lives, it will not take us long to find many things God regards as sinful.

We must humble ourselves, pray and seek His face, and turn from our wicked ways. If we fulfill these three conditions, God responds by promising three things.

- I will hear from heaven
- I will forgive their sins
- I will heal their land.

Our land in this context is our personal lives and the church. Do we need healing? Yes.

Is there a balm in Gilead? Yes, there is—the Lord Jesus. Praise His name!

23

So Great Salvation

I regularly went into Cardiff Prison with the Gospel Male Voice Choir, and on one occasion when it was my turn to give the gospel talk, I chose a subject that afterward I was embarrassed about. It was a warning found in Hebrews 2:3: "How shall we escape if we neglect so great salvation?" I could have been cautioned and even arrested by the prison authorities for incitement to escape.

On another occasion, when I was in my early twenties, I belonged to an a cappella Christian male voice quartet, and we used to preach and sing in many places including a maternity hospital. Once again, it was my turn to speak, and in my naivety, I chose Matthew 11:28: "Come unto me, all ye that labour and are heavy laden, and I will give you rest." Again, how embarrassing!

But this question in Hebrews 2:3 is an important one especially when we consider the plight of unbelievers and the fact that their eternal destiny is at stake.

When we are trying to start a conversation with someone and especially a stranger, we will usually ask questions which have no importance: "Isn't it a nice day?" "How are you?" "What did you think of the football match yesterday?" Christians trusting in the

Lord Jesus for salvation should remember what the Lord saved them from just as David recalled in Psalm 40:2–3.

> He brought me up also out of an horrible pit, out of the miry clay, and set my feet upon a rock, and established my goings. And he hath put a new song in my mouth, even praise unto our God: many shall see it, and fear, and shall trust in the Lord.

I want to look at three words in this text—*escape, neglect,* and *salvation.*

The word *escape* …

On September 11, 2001, three thousand people had gone to the offices in the Twin Towers in New York and no doubt many were engaged in small talk until disaster came. Then they would have had one question: "How shall we escape?" Nothing was as important as that question. Sadly, there was no escape for the majority.

At that time, my son lived in New York. One of his friends worked on a top floor of one of the towers. Only a couple of weeks before the disaster, he had given us a tour of the tower; we did not have to join the long queue as did other tourists. After the disaster, I asked my son what had happened to his friend, and he said that he had left his job there only a week earlier. Mercifully, he had not had to ask, "How shall I escape?"

What are many people trying to escape from? Boredom. Addictions. Financial or health concerns. Family worries. They are not conscious of their greatest need, that of their soul's salvation. God gave His Son; what more can He do? John 3:16–18 reads,

> For God so loved the world, that he gave his only begotten Son, that whosoever believeth in him should not perish, but have everlasting life. For God sent not his Son into the world to condemn

the world; but that the world through him might
be saved.

Without Christ as Savior, there is no escape. Hebrews 10:31 states, "It is a fearful thing to fall into the hands of the living God!"

The second word I want to talk about is *neglect*. How will we escape if we neglect so great a salvation? The results of neglect are usually harmful or even disastrous. For example, we all know about child neglect, and a businessman might lose his business not through illegal means but by simple neglect. Those who are sick can become sicker if they neglect taking their medicines. Many problems occur through neglect of some kind, and the results are usually slow and imperceptible like rust, rot, decay, and mildew.

There are people around us—neighbors, friends, and family— who neglect their souls' salvation. Even believers can neglect their souls by starving them of the Word of God, which is necessary to feed their Christian lives and to grow spiritually.

We must remind ourselves that God holds the key to all things unknown. We may have had many warnings, but they are no good if they are ignored.

The third word is *salvation*, a so great salvation. Praise God if you are one of His children. Why it is a so great salvation?

- Because God is its originator; He was motivated by His great love for humankind.
- Because it frees the sinner from the power, the presence, and the penalty of sin.
- Because of the great cost involved. It cost the life of God's only beloved Son dying on a cross bearing the punishment for our sin. (1 Peter 1:18)
- Because it is universal. It is available to all who put their trust in the Savior.
- Because of the multitude of blessings accompanying salvation not the least of which is becoming a child of God.

24

Stars

Astronomers estimate that in just our Milky Way galaxy alone, there are about three hundred billion stars, and they estimate that there are as many galaxies in the universe.

Christians believe that the stars were created by God and that they demonstrate His great power: "And God made two great lights; the greater light to rule the day, and the lesser light to rule the night: He made the stars also" (Genesis 1:16).

Stars are mentioned frequently in the Bible and particularly at Christmastime. The wise men—philosophers and astronomers who had most likely studied the Old Testament—traveled from Persia or Arabia bearing gifts and followed a special star we call the Star of Bethlehem, which led them to Jesus. Sometimes, we overlook the reaction of the magi in Matthew 2:10: "When they saw the star they rejoiced with exceeding great joy." Among the ancients, the appearance of a new star or comet was regarded as an omen of some remarkable event. Many such appearances are recorded by the Roman historians at the birth or death of someone important. And they say that at the death of Julius Caesar, a comet appeared in the heavens and shone for seven days.

These wise men considered the Star of Bethlehem as evidence

that the long-expected Prince had been born. It is possible that they had been led to this belief by the prophecy of Balaam in Numbers 24:15–17 (TLB).

> Balaam the son of Beor is the man whose eyes are open! He hears the words of God and has knowledge from the Highest; and he sees what the Almighty God has shown him; he fell, and his eyes were opened: [He said] I see in the future of Israel, far down the distant trail, that there shall come a star from Jacob! This ruler of Israel.

They rejoiced because they felt assured that they were under a heavenly guidance and would be conducted to the newborn King of the Jews.

Our being led to Christ should fill us with joy. He is the way, the truth, and the life; our Savior, our friend, our all in all. There is no other way of life, and there is no peace to the soul until He is found. When we are guided to Him, our hearts should overflow with joy and praise.

But I want to mention more stars that should fill us with joy because they all describe the Lord Jesus. In Revelation 22:16, we read that Jesus said, "I am the Bright and Morning Star." In 2 Peter 1:19 Peter wrote, "Ye do well that ye take heed, as unto a light that shineth in a dark place, until the day dawn, and the day star arise in your hearts."

Peter compared the prophetic Word to a light shining in a dark place that gave us light until the new day dawned when Christ, the Day Star, would appear.

One scholar said, 2 Peter 1:12-21

> The world, to Peter, is a dark and murky dungeon. The Word of God is the only dependable light we have in this world. We must heed this Word

111

and not lean on the ideas of men. One day soon, Christ, the Day Star, will arise and take His people home. To the church, Christ is the Day Star that appears when things are the darkest, just before the dawn. (from Wiersbe's Expository Outlines on the New Testament).

In Isaiah 9:2, we read, "The people that walked in darkness have seen a great light: they that dwell in the land of the shadow of death, upon them hath the light shined." This speaks of Jesus, who said, "I am the Light of the world."

The Bright and Morning Star

Venus is the last and brightest star that appears just a few hours before sunrise. It is also called the Day Star. Jesus Christ is "the Bright and Morning Star." Prophetically, His coming is like the morning star, the beginning of a bright new day.

In Revelation 22:15–16, John wrote about the morning star, which announces dawn's imminent arrival. It is a pledge in the sky that a new day is dawning, that Jesus Christ will come for His church as the Morning Star. The light we have is comparatively dim, but there is a day behind it. This is a dark world full of evil, yet things will not always be so. The Lord Jesus has promised to come into the air to take His people home. The darkness of night is an apt description of the present world.

The sight of the Star of Bethlehem caused the magi to rejoice, and as we contemplate the Lord Jesus as the Bright and Morning Star and as the Day Star, it should have the same effect on us. He is the pledge of a bright new day for us when God will wipe away our tears and there will be no more death, sorrow, crying, or pain.

This is the response of a believer.

Looking at that beautiful star, I thought of these sweet words of Jesus: "I am the bright and morning star." The sight of that star made me glad. It gave me joy then, while I was looking at it. And it gives me joy now, whenever I think about it. But all the stars in the world put together are not half so beautiful as Jesus is. And when we see Him, and know Him, as our "bright and Morning Star," there is no joy to be found in anything so great as that which He gives. (From Sermons by R Newton D D in the Biblical Illustrator. Biblesoft.com).

The night is far spent; the day is at hand. (Romans 13:12)

25

Cheer Up!

Someone said, "Cheer up, my friend. God doesn't give us what we can handle; God helps us handle what we are given." Daily life is full of hardship, fear, stress, pain, and so many other things that demoralize us, but God does help us handle what we are given, and that is the wonderful thing about being children of God. He cares for us as a father cares for his children.

> As a father pities his children, so the Lord pities those who fear Him. For He knows our frame; and He remembers that we are dust. (Psalm 103:13–14 NKJV)

The word *pities* occurs 125 times in the Old Testament, where it means "is compassionate" and "merciful." Another verse springs to mind that confirms that God as our heavenly Father does not let us suffer beyond what we can bear. He also gives us a way of escape, just like a pressure valve.

> There hath no temptation [testing] taken you, but such as is common to man: but God is faithful,

who will not suffer you to be tempted [tested] above that ye are able; but will with the temptation also make a way to escape that ye may be able to bear it. (1 Corinthians 10:13)

Do you have reason to be discouraged, disheartened, downhearted, down in the dumps, or sad when you know that our Father in heaven cares for you as much as He does? No. You have every reason to be encouraged and to cheer up.

There are several occasions in scripture when Jesus brought cheer to people in need.

The cheer up of pardon—the forgiveness of sins …

We read of this account in Matthew 9:1–8 (NLT).

Jesus climbed into a boat and went back across the lake to his own town. Some people brought to him a paralyzed man on a mat. Seeing their faith, Jesus said to the paralyzed man, Cheer up, my child! For your sins are forgiven.

But some of the teachers of religious law said to themselves, "That's blasphemy! Does he think he's God?" Jesus knew what they were thinking, so he asked them, why do you have such evil thoughts in your hearts? Is it easier to say, your sins are forgiven, or stand up and walk? So, I will prove to you that the Son of Man has the authority on earth to forgive sins.

Then Jesus turned to the paralyzed man and said, "Stand up, pick up your mat, and go home!" And the man jumped up and went home! Fear swept through the crowd as they saw this happen. And they praised God for sending a man with such great authority.

To have forgiveness of our sins must be a great cause for cheer. Being right with God!

The cheer up of peace—relief from distress ...
We read in Luke 8:41–48 (NKJV),

And behold, there came a man named Jairus, and he was a ruler of the synagogue. And he fell down at Jesus' feet and begged Him to come to his house, for he had an only daughter about twelve years of age, and she was dying.

But as He went, the multitudes thronged Him. Now a woman, having a flow of blood for twelve years, who had spent all her livelihood on physicians and could not be healed by any, came from behind and touched the border of His garment. And immediately her flow of blood stopped. And Jesus said, who touched Me?

When all denied it, Peter, and those with him said, Master, the multitudes throng and press You, and You say, who touched Me? But Jesus said, somebody touched Me, for I perceived power going out from Me.

Now when the woman saw that she was not hidden, she came trembling; and falling down before Him, she declared to Him in the presence of all the people the reason she had touched Him and how she was healed immediately.

And He said to her, "Daughter, be of good cheer; your faith has made you well. Go in peace.

The cheer up of the Lord's presence ...

And straightway He constrained His disciples to get into the ship, and to go to the other side before unto Bethsaida, while He sent away the people. And when He had sent them away, He departed into a mountain to pray. And when even was come, the ship was in the midst of the sea, and He alone on the land. And He saw them toiling in rowing, for the wind was contrary unto them. And about the fourth watch of the night, He cometh unto them, walking upon the sea, and would have passed by them. But when they saw Him walking upon the sea, they supposed it had been a spirit, and cried out, for they all saw Him and were troubled.

And immediately He talked with them, and saith unto them, be of good cheer: it is I; be not afraid. And He went up unto them into the ship; and the wind ceased: and they were sore amazed in themselves beyond measure and wondered. (Mark 6:45–51)

What a comfort to know that when we go through troubled waters and walk through fire, we have the presence of the Lord just as Jesus was with His disciples on the sea.

When you pass through the waters, I will be with you; And through the rivers, they shall not overflow you. When you walk through the fire, you shall not be burned, nor shall the flame

scorch you, for I am the Lord your God, the Holy
One of Israel, your Saviour; fear not, for I am with
you. (Isaiah 43:2–5 NKJV)

The cheer up of power …

These things I have spoken unto you, that in me
ye might have peace. In the world ye shall have
tribulation: but be of good cheer; I have overcome
the world. (John 16:33)

Here, He announced the good cheer of His victory over the
world. We are overcomers because He first overcame for us.

Jesus said that we would have tribulation and troubles, but
the great thing is that He has overcome the world. When we yield
ourselves to Christ and trust Him, He enables us to be overcomers.
We must claim our spiritual position in Christ, in whom we have
victory.

For whatsoever is born of God overcometh the
world: and this is the victory that overcometh the
world, even our faith. Who is he that overcometh
the world, but he that believeth that Jesus is the
Son of God? (1 John 5:4–5)

Believers are either overcome or are overcomers, and "this is
the victory that overcometh the world, even our faith." The world
wants to overcome us; Satan uses the world to persecute and put
pressure on believers. The world wants us to conform; it does not
want us to be different.

So we have seen that "Be of good cheer!" is one of our Lord's
repeated statements of encouragement, which literally means,
"Cheer up!" There is the good cheer of His pardon, peace,
presence, and power.

26

Dwelling on High

Reading: Isaiah 33:15–17 (NASU)

> He who walks righteously [feet] and speaks with sincerity, [mouth]; he who rejects unjust gain [will] and shakes his hands so that they hold no bribe [hands]; he who stops his ears from hearing about bloodshed [ears] and shuts his eyes from looking upon evil [eyes]; He will dwell on the heights; His refuge will be the impregnable rock. His bread will be given him, His water will be sure. Your eyes will see the King in His beauty. They will behold a far-distant land.

These verses give us God's portrait of a man or woman of God, the Christian, but not so much about the inner person but the outward person. They describe how we should conduct ourselves. They concern every part of our lives of witness before the world.

The Christian life touches the whole life—feet, mouth, will, hands, ears, and eyes. Verse 15 describes the one who dwells on high as one who walks righteously and speaks uprightly who rejects gain from extortion, keeps his hand from accepting bribes, stops his ears from hearing of blood, and shuts his eyes to evil. In these days of lockdown, we are constantly reminded to clean our hands lest we contract the deadly virus.

In Romans 6:12–18 (NLT), Paul wrote,

> Do not let sin control the way you live; do not give in to sinful desires. Do not let any part of your body become an instrument of evil to serve sin. Instead, give yourselves completely to God, for you were dead, but now you have new life. So, use your whole body as an instrument to do what is right for the glory of God. Sin is no longer your master, for you no longer live under the requirements of the law. Instead, you live under the freedom of God's grace.
>
> Well then, since God's grace has set us free from the law, does that mean we can go on sinning? Of course not! Don't you realize that you become the slave of whatever you choose to obey? You can be a slave to sin, which leads to death, or you can choose to obey God, which leads to righteous living. Thank God! Once you were slaves of sin, but now you wholeheartedly obey this teaching we have given you. Now you are free from your slavery to sin, and you have become slaves to righteous living.

Isaiah 33 (NASU) mentions some of the Christians' privileges relating to their position, protection, provision, and prospect.

Our position "shall dwell on the heights" …

This is our position in Christ. In Ephesians 2:6, we read, "He has made us to sit together in heavenly places in Christ Jesus." And in Ephesians 1:3–7, Paul wrote,

> Blessed be the God and Father of our Lord Jesus Christ, who hath blessed us with all spiritual blessings in heavenly places in Christ: According as he hath chosen us in Him before the foundation of the world, that we should be holy and without blame before Him in love: Having predestined us unto the adoption of children by Jesus Christ to himself, according to the good pleasure of his will, to the praise of the glory of his grace, wherein he hath made us accepted in the beloved. In whom we have redemption through his blood, the forgiveness of sins, according to the riches of his grace.

Should we ever be discouraged?
Our protection as believers in Christ …

> His place of defence shall be in the munitions of rocks. (v. 16)

> When my heart is overwhelmed: lead me to the rock that is higher than I. For thou hast been a shelter for me, and a strong tower from the enemy. [Christ is that Rock]. (Psalm 61:2–3)

> And I give unto them eternal life; and they shall never perish, neither shall any man pluck them out of my hand. My Father, which gave them me, is greater than all; and no man is able to pluck them out of my Father's hand. (John 10:28–29)

Our provision as believers in Christ …

> Bread shall be given him; his waters shall be sure.
> (v. 16)

I shall not want [lack anything]. (Psalm 23)

> The young lions do lack, and suffer hunger, but
> they that seek the Lord shall not lack any good
> thing. (Psalm 34:10)

> And it is he who will supply all your needs from
> his riches in glory because of what Christ Jesus
> has done for us. Now unto God our Father be
> glory forever and ever. Amen. (Philippians 4:19–
> 20 TLB)

We sing in Charles Wesley's hymn "Jesus, Lover of My Soul,"
"Thou, O Christ art all I want; more than all in Thee I find."
Our prospect as believers in Christ …

> Thine eyes shall see the King in His beauty; they
> shall behold the land that is very far off. (v. 17)

Job had this confidence; we read in Job 19:26–27,

> Though after my skin worms destroy this body,
> yet in my flesh shall I see God, Whom I shall see
> for myself, and mine eyes shall behold, and not
> another.

> One thing have I desired of the Lord … to behold
> the beauty of the Lord. (Psalm 27:4)

Beloved, now are we the sons of God, and it doth not yet appear what we shall be: but we know that, when he shall appear, we shall be like him; for we shall see him as he is. (1 John 3:2)

As children of God, we have the wonderful prospect of one day seeing the King, the Lord Jesus, in all His beauty; the One of whom it could once be said, "we saw no beauty in Him that we should desire Him". (Isaiah 53:2)

But there is more in prospect. "They shall behold the land that is very far off." It says of the heroes of faith in Hebrews 11:13–14,

Not having received the promises, but having seen them afar off, and were persuaded of them, and embraced them, and confessed that they were strangers and pilgrims on the earth. For they that say such things declare plainly that they seek a country.

The Bible is like a map, guiding us through life's journey and sometimes it warns us of perilous places of danger. It is also like a telescope enabling us to see things not available to the naked eye. Sailors heading for shipwreck use their telescopes to guide them through the dangerous seas. They focus on the land ahead, and they cry with relief "land ahoy!" Look for the country that is beyond, and the prospect of standing on its shore. It will help you to rejoice despite your light affliction, which is but for a moment

Acts 27:5–8 tells of the dangerous voyage Paul and his companions made by ship from Caesarea to Rome. It was Paul's third and final missionary journey.

> When we had sailed over the sea of Cilicia and Pamphylia, we came to Myra, a city of Lycia. And there the centurion found a ship from Alexandria sailing into Italy; and he put us therein. And when we had sailed slowly many days, and scarce were come over against Cnidus, the wind not suffering us, we sailed under Crete, over against Salmone; And, hardly passing it, came unto a place which is called the fair havens; nigh whereunto was the city of Lasea.

Although in danger of shipwreck near the city of Lasea, the captain must have spotted land and safety, and they came into the harbor called Fair Havens. What a relief!

The harbor still exists; it is Kali Limenes, Greek for "Fair Havens." It is on the southern coast of Crete, and its position matches the biblical description.

I often visited a home for the elderly near my hometown with friends, and we sang and preached the gospel to the residents every fortnight for many years. The name of the home was Fair Haven. What a lovely haven of rest and safety for the elderly to spend on their final journey to glory.

What a wonderful Savior we have as we think of all our privileges He has graciously given us. By His grace, we have our position dwelling on high, the protection He gives, safety in the Rock of Ages, our provision for He supplies all our needs, and our prospect of seeing the King in all His beauty and heading for the place He has gone to prepare for us in a land that is very far off.

Suffering and Glory

27

Some of my favorite biblical verses are in 2 Corinthians 4:16–5:1 (NKJV)

> Therefore, we do not lose heart. Even though our outward man is perishing, yet the inward man is being renewed day by day. For our light affliction, which is but for a moment, is working for us a far more exceeding and eternal weight of glory, while we do not look at the things which are seen, but at the things which are not seen.

> For the things which are seen are temporary, but the things which are not seen are eternal. For we know that if our earthly house, this tent, is destroyed, we have a building from God, a house not made with hands, eternal in the heavens.

Paul, who had experienced much hardship for the name of Christ, seemed to be stating a principle to encourage believers who were suffering that would in the end bring glory. This principle seems to be repeated in various other scriptures.

> If children, then heirs; heirs of God, and joint heirs with Christ; if so be that we suffer with him, that we may be also glorified together. For I reckon that the sufferings of this present time are not worthy to be compared with the glory which shall be revealed in us. (Romans 8:17–18)

Peter mentioned this in his first letter with reference to the Old Testament prophets who foretold the coming of the Messiah testifying of "the sufferings of Christ and the glory that should follow" (1 Peter 1:11).

Jesus Himself asked the two disciples in Emmaus, "Ought not Christ to have suffered these things and to enter into His glory?" (Luke 24:26).

In Hebrews 12:2, we read that Jesus "endured the Cross for the joy that was set before Him," meaning that He saw beyond the agony and suffering of the cross and anticipated the glory that was to follow.

> But we see Jesus, who was made a little lower than the angels for the suffering of death, crowned with glory and honour. (Hebrews 2:9)

> If we suffer, we shall also reign with him.
> (2 Timothy 2:12)

> For it became him, for whom are all things, and by whom are all things, in bringing many sons unto glory, to make the captain of their salvation perfect through the sufferings. (Hebrews 2:10)

These scriptures tell us that suffering for Christ does not mean defeat but rather victory and glory.

> We do not lose heart; even though our outward man is perishing, yet the inward man is being renewed day by day, for our light affliction, which is but for a moment, is working for us a far more exceeding and eternal weight of glory. (2 Corinthians 4:16 NKJV)

The NLT puts it this way.

> That is why we never give up. Though our bodies are dying, our spirits are being renewed every day. For our present troubles are small and won't last very long. Yet they produce for us a glory that vastly outweighs them and will last forever!

Our light affliction, says Paul … What? It was no light affliction that Paul and his companions suffered—shipwrecks, famine, beatings, and imprisonments. They were heavy burdens to bear, and we must not detract from the severity of the sufferings of Paul and his companions. Paul was using the method of comparison. Compared to a football, the earth is huge, but compared to the sun, it is tiny. In this verse, Paul was talking about weight, not size; a ton of coal is so much greater than a pound of sugar, which is so much greater than a single granule of sugar. In our eyes, our suffering and pain are not little, but they are when compared with the glory that will follow. That is why Paul said we were not to lose heart, faint, or give up. "Wherefore lift up the hands which hang down, and the feeble knees" (Hebrews 12:12).

That is why I am describing this light affliction as trivial, transitory, transforming, and triumphant. When compared with the weight of glory God has promised us, this light affliction is trivial. It is also transient; it is "but for a moment." You may have been suffering from arthritis for years, but that is temporary when compared with the eternal bliss God has promised you.

Our afflictions are transforming because they are "working for us." They are productive. Often, we suffer as the result of our willfulness and rebellion and bring suffering upon ourselves. But in the case of believers, their pain and suffering may be God's purpose to make them into the persons He wants us to be. God is working to mould our character.

Our sufferings are triumphant because they produce for us "a far more exceeding weight of glory." This glory is an eternal home in heaven, where we will see the Lord and become like Him. I recoil sometimes at the prospect that I should ever receive any reward or glory especially when I sing "That Will Be Glory for Me." And my mind turns to Psalm 115:1: "Not unto us, O Lord, not unto us, but unto thy name give glory, for thy mercy, and for thy truth's sake." But then I remember there is intrinsic glory that belongs to the Lord, and there is glory being reflected from somebody else, from the Lord to you and me. Moses's face shone with reflected glory when he came down from Mount Sinai having received the Ten Commandments.

> And the glory which thou gavest me I have given them; that they may be one, even as we are one: I in them, and thou in me, that they may be made perfect in one; and that the world may know that thou hast sent me, and hast loved them, as thou hast loved me. Father, I will that they also, whom thou hast given me, be with me where I am; that they may behold my glory, which thou hast given me: for thou lovedst me before the foundation of the world. (John 17:22–24)

And I John saw the holy city, new Jerusalem, coming down from God out of heaven, prepared as a bride adorned for her husband ... And God shall wipe away all tears from their eyes; and there shall be no more death, neither sorrow, nor crying, neither shall there be any more pain: for the former things are passed away. And he that sat upon the throne said, Behold, I make all things new. (Revelation 21:2–5)

Blessed be the God and Father of our Lord Jesus Christ, who according to His abundant mercy has begotten us again to a living hope through the resurrection of Jesus Christ from the dead to an inheritance incorruptible and undefiled and that does not fade away, reserved in heaven for you, who are kept by the power of God through faith for salvation ready to be revealed in the last time. (1 Peter 1:3–5)

Toward the end of his life, Paul wrote in 2 Timothy 4:7–8 (NIV),

I have fought the good fight, I have finished the race, I have kept the faith. Now there is in store for me the crown of righteousness, which the Lord, the righteous Judge, will award to me on that day—and not only to me, but also to all who have longed for His appearing.

28

Come and See

There are times when Jesus wants to show us something new: Come and see what happens when you talk about Me to your friends. Come and see what you will learn if you commit to that Bible study. Come and see how I can use you if you commit your life fully to Me. Come and see how close we can be when you start each day in prayer.

His invitation is being extended to us all now. How will we respond?

The Homeless Man

Come and see where He dwells on earth (John 1:38–39). One day, when Andrew and another disciple were following Jesus and listening to His conversation, Jesus asked them what they wanted. They said, "Master, where dwellest thou?" And Jesus replied, "Come and see." Where did Jesus take them? Wherever it was the Bible says, they stayed with Him for that day. Was it in the mountains? We don't know. But we do know that Jesus had no regular place to call home though I guess He lived with his parents in Nazareth before

He commenced His public ministry. He often went to a mountain. We read in John 6:15 that He went to a mountain alone.

He is often known as the homeless stranger. The reply of Jesus to come and see is intriguing to us believers because the scriptures tell us that a certain scribe came to Jesus on another occasion and said, "'Master, I will follow You wherever You go.' And Jesus told him, 'The foxes have holes, and the birds of the air have nests; but the Son of man hath not where to lay his head'" (Matthew 8:19–20).

The Heavenly Man

Come and see where His eternal home is. It is amazing to think that the Son of God, who was homeless in this world, dwelt in the bosom of the Father. John said, "the only begotten Son, which is in the bosom of the Father" (John 1:18), and who as Paul recorded was dwelling "in the light which no man can approach unto" (1 Timothy 6:16). He is "the high and lofty One that inhabits eternity, whose name is Holy" (Isaiah 57:15). He is the heavenly man. So often, He told His disciples that He "came down from heaven."

How wonderful to think that He came down as the Word of God to dwell among us. (John 1:14) and be our Savior. He came out of the ivory palaces into this world of woe (Psalm 45:8).

Jesus was not known as the Son of Man until He took on manhood at His birth.

> Who [Christ], being in the form of God, thought it not robbery to be equal with God but made himself of no reputation, and took upon him the form of a servant, and was made in the likeness of men; and being found in fashion as a man, he humbled

himself, and became obedient unto death, even the death of the cross. (Philippians 2:6–8)

And no man hath ascended up to heaven, but he that came down from heaven, even the Son of man which is in heaven. (John 3:13)

For I came down from heaven, not to do mine own will, but the will of him that sent me. (John 6:38)

I am the living bread which came down from heaven: if any man eat of this bread, he shall live for ever: and the bread that I will give is my flesh, which I will give for the life of the world. (John 6:51)

Your father Abraham rejoiced to see my day: and he saw it and was glad. Then said the Jews unto him, Thou art not yet fifty years old, and hast thou seen Abraham? Jesus said unto them, Verily, verily, I say unto you, Before Abraham was, I am. (John 8:56–58)

We have seen and do testify that the Father sent the Son to be the Saviour of the world. (1 John 4:14)

The Indwelling Man

"That Christ may dwell in your hearts by faith." It is marvelous enough that He should come down from heaven to dwell with us, but it is even more wonderful that He dwells in believers. Jesus told His disciples that the Comforter would not only be with them but that He would also be in them (John 14:17).

Paul's desire for the Ephesian believers was "That Christ may dwell in your hearts by faith; that ye, being rooted and grounded in love....." (Ephesians 3:17).

To dwell is to be at home, to be in your hearts; to live in your innermost being. (Vine's Expository Dictionary of NT words).

I think of the heart as the control center, and Christ wants to be in the control center of our lives.

It is a mystery to us that Christ should dwell in us. Paul expressed it in this way in Colossians 1:27: "To whom God would make known what the riches of the glory of this mystery is among the Gentiles, which is Christ in you, the hope of glory."

The Promised Man

> Philip found Nathanael and said to him, we have found Him of whom Moses in the law, and the prophets, wrote—Jesus of Nazareth, the son of Joseph. And Nathanael said to him, can anything good come out of Nazareth? Philip said to him, Come and see. (John 1:45–46 NKJV)

The woman of Samaria said to her neighbors, "Come, see a man, which told me all things that ever I did: is not this the Christ?" (John 4:29). How wonderful we can say that we have found Him.

The Risen Man

> Come, see the place where the Lord lay. (Matthew 28:6)

Early in the morning on the first day of the week after Jesus had been crucified and laid in the tomb, there was an earthquake, and an angel rolled the stone away from the entrance of the tomb. Mary Magdalene and another Mary came to visit the tomb and found the stone rolled away. They were quite shaken, but the angel said to the women,

> Fear not ye: for I know that ye seek Jesus, which was crucified. He is not here: for he is risen, as He said. Come, see the place where the Lord lay. And go quickly and tell His disciples that He is risen from the dead; and behold, He goeth before you into Galilee; there shall ye see Him: lo, I have told you. (Matthew 28:5–7)

Jesus asked Mary the same question when Lazarus had died: "Where have ye laid him? They said unto him, Lord, come and see. Jesus wept. Then said the Jews, behold how he loved him!" (John 11:34–36).

Lazarus, how sad! A body in the grave. Jesus, how glad! No body in the grave.

The Supreme Man

Come and see the great works of God.

> Come and see what God has done; He is awesome in his deeds toward the children of men. (Psalm 66:5 ESV)

> But we see Jesus, who was made a little lower than the angels for the suffering of death, crowned with glory and honour; that he by the grace of God should taste death for every man. (Hebrews 2:9)

29

The Three Bears

This is not the Goldilocks story. I'm going to talk about the three bears in Galatians 6. In verse 1, Paul gave some practical teaching on how to deal with a fellow believer who had fallen into sin. He was saying that they should deal gently with him with a view to restoring him. This led Paul to state the principle involved: "Bear ye one another's burdens" (v. 2).

How many in today's pressurized times are bearing burdens of one kind or another? The burdens may be of many kinds—health problems, financial worries, family troubles, wayward children, marital difficulties, bereavement, loneliness, frailty, and now the coronavirus. The list is endless.

We know there are many situations where our brothers and sisters are carrying burdens that are hard to bear, and it is our responsibility to help them bear the weight. You might ask why you should bear another's burden. They could be in trouble because of their own fault. On the other hand, their problems may have arisen from circumstances beyond their control. What are we to do as Christians? Walk by on the other side like the priest and the Levite in the story of the Good Samaritan? Or come to where our needy friends are and show compassion and give relief?

Paul is consistent in his ministry; we read in Romans 15:1–3 (ASV),

> Now we that are strong ought to bear the infirmities of the weak, and not to please ourselves. Let each one of us please his neighbour for the good, unto edifying. For Christ also pleased not himself.

Jesus saw us bruised by sin and in our helplessness heading for a lost eternity, and He came from heaven to where we were just like the Good Samaritan to show us the love of God by bearing the heavy load of our sin and dying on the cross.

Bearing one another's burdens does not mean that the Lord will not carry our burdens when the going gets too tough. We do not have to carry our burdens alone, and even though we may share our burdens with other believers, we can still bring them to the Lord Jesus Christ, who gives rest to the weary and heavy laden.

The psalmist David encouraged us to "cast thy burden upon the Lord, and he shall sustain thee" (Psalm 55:22). And Peter gave this wise counsel: "Casting all your care upon Him; For He careth for you" (1 Peter 5:7).

Those who know the Lord Jesus Christ as their Savior can know relief from the burdens life puts on them. Why do we shoulder those burdens a single day longer when we can bring them to Him now, seek His face in prayer, and experience His grace? We should take confidence in the fact that Jesus does not allow our burdens and testings to weigh us down. Matthew 11:28–30 reads,

> Come unto me, all ye that labour and are heavy laden, and I will give you rest. Take my yoke upon you and learn of me; for I am meek and lowly in heart: and ye shall find rest unto your souls. For my yoke is easy, and my burden is light.

He also said that God could be trusted to make a way we can bear our burdens.

> Therefore, let him who thinks he stands take heed lest he fall. No temptation has overtaken you except such as is common to man; but God is faithful, who will not allow you to be tempted beyond what you are able, but with the temptation will also make the way of escape, that you may be able to bear it. (1 Corinthians 10:12–13)

God provided manna for the children of Israel in the wilderness, but the people began to grumble; they wanted meat as well. In Numbers 11:10–17 (NLT) is the record of how Moses complained to God that he could not bear the burden and how God's solution was that Moses should share the burden with seventy of the elders of Israel.

> Moses heard all the families standing in the doorways of their tents whining, and the Lord became extremely angry. Moses was also very aggravated. And Moses said to the Lord, how can I carry them to the land you swore to give their ancestors? Where am I supposed to get meat for all these people? They keep whining to me, saying, "Give us meat to eat!' I can't carry all these people by myself! The load is far too heavy! If this is how you intend to treat me, just go ahead, and kill me." Do me a favor and spare me this misery!
>
> Then the Lord said to Moses, gather before me seventy men who are recognized as elders and leaders of Israel. Bring them to the tabernacle to stand there with you. I will come down and talk

to you there. I will take some of the Spirit that is
upon you, and I will put the Spirit upon them
also. They will bear the burden of the people
along with you, so you will not have to carry it
alone.

How wonderful! The Lord has His eye on us all the time. He
is our refuge and strength, a very present help. He will not allow
us to sink beneath the heavy load we may be struggling with.

Did you grasp the full meaning of what Paul was saying?
"Bear each other's burdens." In other words, it is a two-way thing.
You might say that you are always ready to help others, but Paul
was asking, "Are you happy for someone to help you?" Some
people would rather not share their burdens as they consider them
a personal matter, but a preacher once said that there should be no
such thing as "My personal life is none of your business."

It is sad if we cannot share our burdens because we all belong
to the same family, and we should love and care for each other.
According to 1 Corinthians 12, we are members of the one body,
and if one member cannot function as it should, the whole body
will be affected, and its testimony and effectiveness may suffer.

Unfortunately, we do not attend a perfect church, and
consequently, two things may prevent us from sharing our
burdens—pride and gossip. If only we could banish these two
things from our lives. Let us examine ourselves to see if there is
pride there and make sure we do not gossip and thus cause hurt
and possibly division in the church.

We often see on TV heartbreaking situations in Africa.
Often, children whose parents have been killed in fighting
against terrorists are fending for themselves and taking on the
responsibilities of adults. Often, two children will be seen, one
carrying the other on his back sometimes through the desert
or rough country. Not long afterward, they stop and exchange

places. They carry each other in turn. That is bearing each other's burdens.

A similar situation inspired the writing of a pop song by the Hollies and popularized by Neil Diamond, a pop singer of the 1960s. "He Ain't Heavy; He's My Brother." Yes, he was heavy, but the brother was not going to be put off by the weight; he shouldered the burden gladly without complaint, and so should we.

Paul gave a reason for the principle: "And so, fulfil the law of Christ" (Galatians 6:2). When we bear each other's burdens, we fulfill the law of Christ. In his letter, James mentioned the royal law and recalled Jesus's words in John 13:34: "A new commandment I give unto you, that you love one another; as I have loved you, that ye love one another." When we bear one another's burdens, we are practicing and showing the love of Christ.

Then we come to the second bear in verse 5: "Every man shall bear his own burden." This seems to contradict what we have just been saying, but it is not a contradiction. The word for burden here is a different Greek word meaning something to be carried and not a heavy weight. What Paul was saying was that there was something to carry that we cannot shelve or pass on to someone else. It is entirely our own personal responsibility. What is it?

Verses 3 and 4 give us the clue. The NIV renders this as,

> If anyone thinks he is something when he is nothing, he deceives himself. Each one should test his own actions. Then he can take pride in himself without comparing himself to somebody else.

In verse 3, we have self-deception, and in verse 4, we have self-examination. This implies that we have a personal responsibility to make sure we do not deceive ourselves into thinking we are self-sufficient and do not need our brothers and sisters. And we should not be so proud as to think we are above helping others or indeed above needing others' help. We deceive ourselves if we think we do not need each other. Verse 4 is telling us to check our own progress in the Christian life and not compare ourselves with others.

The third bear is in verse 17, where Paul says, "I bear in my body the marks of the Lord Jesus." Paul was comparing the scars made by circumcision with the marks of the scourging and beatings and other hardships he suffered for preaching the gospel. If the Galatians had any doubts about Paul's devotion to Christ, these marks on his body and the scars he suffered for the sake of his Savior spoke more eloquently than the marks made by circumcision. These marks are literally brand marks, marks burned into the flesh of a slave by his master and as the branding of cattle. The marks are proof of ownership. What marks do we bear that demonstrate our devotion to the Lord Jesus? More pointedly, do we bear any marks? Do our friends and neighbors see any marks? I don't mean physical marks except for a smile. Many Christians in other countries are being beaten, imprisoned, and killed for the sake of Christ.

What should be the marks of a true believer? The Bible tells us of the fruit of the Spirit: "The fruit of the Spirit is love, joy, peace, longsuffering, gentleness, goodness, faith, meekness, temperance" (Galatians 5:22–23).

Jesus said, "By this shall all men know that you are My disciples, if you have love one to another" (John 13:35).

Is there enough proof in our lives to show that we are the bond slaves of the Lord Jesus, that we belong to Him? Or do we bear the marks of the world?

I hope you will remember these three bears.

1. Bear each other's burdens. (v. 2)
2. Bear your burden of responsibility. (v. 5)
3. Bear the marks of Christ's ownership. (v. 17)

Someone bore a burden no other person could have borne and has the marks on His body to prove it. Of course, I am referring to the Lord Jesus.

> He Himself bore our sins in His body on the cross, so that we might die to sin and live to righteousness. For by His wounds you were healed. (1 Peter 2:24 NASU)

30

Birds in the Bible

Ever since Adam and Eve sinned, God's perfect creation was spoiling as the ground was cursed. We are all too conscious of this deterioration today with talk of animals and birds becoming extinct and with fires, floods, and earthquakes not to mention the effects of global warming and now the coronavirus rampaging through the world.

Have you noticed how there seems to be more birds in the garden as well as butterflies now that air pollution has been reduced during the lockdown and especially with the massive reduction of airplanes polluting the atmosphere? Many people now realize what beauty there is even though marred in God's creation as they look out their windows. Illness helps us appreciate the wonders of God's creation.

Thirty years ago, after I came out of hospital, my perspective on life was changed. About that time, there was a popular song, "Little Things Mean a Lot." It is quite true that little things mean a lot more to me now. I used to watch birds in my garden to the extent that I bought binoculars to observe them more closely, and I began painting zebras, deer, and kingfishers with acrylic paints.

Here are some lessons we learn from birds in the Bible.

The Sparrow

Some verses in the Bible speak of sparrows.

> Jesus said, are not two sparrows sold for a farthing? and one of them shall not fall on the ground without your Father [knowing]. But the very hairs of your head are all numbered. Fear ye not therefore, ye are of more value than many sparrows. (Matthew 10:29–31)

Not one of them is forgotten before God. (Luke 12:6)

The Raven

Jesus told His disciples not to worry about where their next meal would come from or what to wear; God would provide those things just as He provided food for the raven and her young.

> Do not worry about your life, what you will eat; nor about the body, what you will put on. Life is more than food, and the body is more than clothing. Consider the ravens, for they neither sow nor reap, which have neither storehouse nor barn; and God feeds them. (Luke 12:22–25 NASU)

Think of some other birds in the Bible that could be regarded as types of the Lord.

The Eagle

Moses seems to have had a good knowledge of nature, and he wrote about eagles and their care for their eaglets; he likened them to the care God had for His people through the wilderness journey.

> As an eagle stirreth up her nest, fluttereth over her young, spreadeth abroad her wings, taketh them, beareth them on her wings: So, the Lord alone did lead him [His people Israel]. (Deuteronomy 32:11–12)

To encourage her fledglings to fly, the mother eagle would flutter a few feet above them. She would also stir up the nest to make it uncomfortable so that they might be more inclined to leave the nest. Then she would push the eaglets to the edge of the nest until they fell out. You might think that was cruel, but the mother would fly out of the nest with her wings outstretched and would soar beneath her young offspring, which would then be carried on her wings.

God reminds His children of how much He cares for them as recorded in Exodus 19:4 (NIV): "You yourselves have seen what I did to Egypt, and how I carried you on eagles' wings and brought you to myself."

One day on a visit to our son's family in Denver, we were walking through a park and saw a crowd staring at a branch of a large tree. There was a bald eagle, the proud national bird symbol of the United States. We walked around the lake and came back to the same spot, and the eagle was still there majestically perched on the same branch.

Sadly, we read about the rebellious and idolatrous nature of God's chosen people in ancient times and how they were taken captive into Assyria. In Micah 1:16, we read how the nation was to be shamed, how its people should suffer great grief and be brought down in weakness before their enemies. Micah referred to the baldness of the eagle and how the molting of its feathers made it weak. In those days, men would cut their long hair to signify great grief and shame, and in this way, Micah likened the people to the bald eagle because they were weak against their enemies, who had taken them into captivity.

> Make thee bald, enlarge thy baldness as the eagle; for they are gone into captivity from thee. (Micah 1:16 ASV)

Was that a picture of the children of Israel as God intended them to be? The day would come when God's people would be restored, and Isaiah gave us a glimpse of that day.

> He giveth power to the faint; and to them that have no might he increaseth strength. Even the youths shall faint and be weary, and the young men shall utterly fall: But they that wait upon the Lord shall renew their strength; they shall mount up with wings as eagles; they shall run, and not be weary; and they shall walk, and not faint. (Isaiah 40:29–31)

Surely, we can say that He has cared for each of us and that we have soared with wings as eagles to the heights of God's blessings.

The Hen

Jesus likened Himself to a hen as He looked over Jerusalem and wept for the town. Its people had missed their opportunity to accept Him as their Messiah, and that caused Him much grief, enough for Him to weep for them. He showed how much He cared for them when He said,

> O Jerusalem, Jerusalem, the one who kills the prophets and stones those who are sent to her! How

often I wanted to gather your children together, as
a hen gathers her brood under her wings, but you
were not willing! (Luke 13:34 NKJV)

The Dove

The white dove is undoubtedly an important bird in the Bible
since it most famously represents the Holy Spirit.

And Jesus, when he was baptized, went up
straightway out of the water: and, lo, the heavens
were opened unto him, and he saw the Spirit of
God descending like a dove, and lighting upon
him. And lo, a voice from heaven, saying, This
is my beloved Son, in whom I am well pleased.
(Matthew 3:16–17)

A dove also symbolizes innocence, purity, and peace.
Throughout the Bible, it is seen to represent only the positive.
These are the words of David.

My heart is sore pained within me: and the terrors
of death are fallen upon me. Fearfulness and
trembling are come upon me, and horror hath
overwhelmed me. And I said, Oh that I had wings
like a dove! for then would I fly away and be at
rest. (Psalm 55:4–6)

And this was Noah's experience of the dove.

And the dove came in to him in the evening; and,
lo, in her mouth was an olive leaf plucked off: so,
Noah knew that the waters were abated from off
the earth. (Genesis 8:11)

Some other small creatures are mentioned in the Bible that might teach us some wise lessons such as the ant and the spider mentioned in Proverbs 30:25: "The ants are a people not strong, yet they prepare their meat in the summer" and verse 28: "The spider taketh hold with her hands and is in kings' palaces."

How often have you brushed aside a cobweb only to find that the spider has woven another one as soon as you have turned your back? Do you remember the legend of Robert the Bruce, who later became the king of Scotland after defeating the English at the famous Battle of Bannockburn? Prior to that battle, he had lost earlier ones and could easily have abandoned his ambition, which was to unite the Scots and set up his kingdom.

He was hiding in a cave when he saw a spider attempting to weave a web, and several times, the spider fell and had to climb back up to complete the web. That taught Robert the lessons of perseverance and endurance. "If at first you don't succeed, try, try again" has become a well-known adage.

In a sense, these small creatures represent us.

- The sparrow: how much God cares for us
- The ant: how we should be wise and prepare for eternity
- The spider: how we should persevere and not give up.

Of how much more value are you than the birds? And which of you by worrying can add one cubit to his stature? (Luke 12:24 NKJV).

31

Beautiful Feet

There is an incident in the Old Testament in the days of Elisha the prophet when the Syrian armies had besieged the city of Samaria as COVID-19 is besieging us today.

> There was a famine in the land and people were dying of starvation. King Jehoram blamed God for the situation, and determined to have Elisha, the man of God, executed. Whereupon Elisha told the King that the Lord would solve the crisis and there would be food on the next day. (2 Kings 7:3–11)

Four lepers outside the gates of Samaria were perishing from hunger, so they decided they could do no worse than go to the camp of the Syrian army. At worst, they would be killed, but they would die anyway of starvation, and there was a chance that they would be given food. To their amazement, when they went into the camp, they found that it had been deserted. God had caused the sounds of chariots and horses to be heard in the night, and the Syrians thought that the king of Israel had enlisted the help of the

Hittites and the Egyptians and had thus fled leaving everything behind.

They could not believe their eyes. They were able to satisfy their hunger and thirst, put on new clothes, and pick up silver and gold. Soon however, their consciences began to prick them as they thought of all the starving souls in the city. They wondered if they should keep the secret to themselves or share it with the needy in the city. They said one to another, "We do not well: this day is a day of good tidings, and we hold our peace" (2 Kings 7:9).

They decided to tell the good news to the gatekeepers of the city, and as a result, all the inhabitants of the city were saved. The word of Elisha was true. God could be trusted. We are in the day of good news, and we know the secret of it, and we do not well if we do not share the good news. Here is a passage from Romans 10:12–16 (NKJV).

> Whoever calls on the name of the Lord shall be saved. How then shall they call on Him in whom they have not believed? And how shall they believe in Him of whom they have not heard? And how shall they hear without a preacher? And how shall they preach unless they are sent? As it is written: "How beautiful are the feet of those who preach the gospel of peace, who bring glad tidings of good things!

The greatest evangelizer in the New Testament was Paul. Wherever he went, people were saved Jews and Gentiles alike. He enthused new converts with such zeal that they were accused of "turning the world upside down." Paul knew that the preaching of the gospel was a necessity, a privilege, and a responsibility.

It is a necessity because it was the commission Jesus gave His disciples: "Go ye into all the world and preach the gospel to every creature" (Mark 16:15). And even, as recorded in Matthew

28:18–20, if only done out of a sense of duty, we should do it as an act of obedience. It is no wonder that Paul said, "Necessity is laid upon me; yea, woe is unto me, if I do not preach the Gospel!" (1 Corinthians 9:16).

The preaching of the gospel is also a privilege. The Bible describes believers as saints, coworkers with God, stewards, servants, ambassadors, and witnesses. Whatever task we undertake in the service of the Lord, we should remember we are not left on our own, that we are coworkers with God. What a privilege to represent the Lord in these capacities. We must not denigrate or belittle this privilege with a carefree attitude, and we must feel our responsibility to God to fulfill our duty bearing in mind that the message of the gospel we proclaim is the power of God.

Before He ascended into heaven, Jesus told His disciples,

> But ye shall receive power, after the Holy Ghost is come upon you: and ye shall be witnesses unto me in Jerusalem, and in all Judaea, in Samaria, and unto the uttermost part of the earth. (Acts 1:8)

Jesus also said in Matthew 28:18–20,

> All power is given unto me in heaven and in earth. Go ye therefore, and teach all nations, baptizing them in the name of the Father, and of the Son, and of the Holy Ghost: Teaching them to observe all things whatsoever I have commanded you: and, lo, I am with you alway, even unto the end of the world. Amen.

In 2 Corinthians 6:1 (NLT), the apostle referred to the responsibility of the coworkers: "As God's partners, we beg you not to accept this marvellous gift of God's kindness and then ignore it."

Many poets have written about unrequited love. As Jesus wept over Jerusalem, I wonder whether it was due to unrequited love. Jerusalem had spurned His love. I know heaven is a place where there is no crying or tears, but I wonder if tears are shed in heaven because of sinners on this earth who reject the Savior.

Christ's love inspires us to spread the good news. As Paul said, "Christ's love compels us" (2 Corinthians 5:14 NIV).

The Pilgrim Preachers was a band of Christian men who went everywhere preaching the gospel during the end of the nineteenth century and well into the twentieth century. Gypsy (Rodney) Smith was one of them in the late 1880s until 1930 as were some preachers from South Wales. It was said of Gypsy Smith that he was in the mould of Billy Graham.

On one of the visits of the Pilgrim Preachers to Glasgow, Dan Kerr, who was driving the preachers around, had to apply for petrol vouchers, and he recalled how the man issuing the vouchers said to him, "You have no need to come to the city of Glasgow," to which Dan replied, "Oh yes, there is a need. Your city's motto says, 'Let Glasgow Flourish by the Preaching of the Word,' except the latter part of the motto has been left out."

Do you ever think of feet as being beautiful? With bunions and verrucas? Well, God does. He described the feet of the evangelist as beautiful.

> How beautiful upon the mountains are the feet of him who brings good news, who proclaims peace, who brings glad tidings of good things, who proclaims salvation, who says to Zion, Your God reigns! (Isaiah 52:7 NKJV)

32

Faces

What's in a word? And what's in a face? Some say that there are six facial expressions: neutrality, happiness, sadness, disgust, fear, and anger. There must be more. Can you think of any?

People make instant judgments about others' characters, ages, health, and moods by their facial expressions. Sometimes they are right, but we know that beauty is different in that it's only skin deep. Helen of Troy was said to have been so beautiful that when she was abducted, a fleet of a thousand ships set sail to win her back from Paris sparking the Trojan War. Mona Lisa, painted over five hundred years ago by Leonardo da Vinci, had an enigmatic smile that has intrigued the world for centuries.

An Unseen Face

It is intriguing to think that no one has seen the face of God. In Exodus 33:20, God said, "Thou canst not see my face: for there shall no man see me, and live." When Moses asked God to show him His glory, God in effect replied, "I will be everything for you. I will be kind, gracious, and show you mercy, but you cannot see My face."

Moses said, I beseech thee, shew to me thy glory. And he [God] said, I will make all my goodness pass before thee, and I will proclaim the name of the Lord before thee; and will be gracious to whom I will be gracious and will shew mercy on whom I will shew mercy. And he said, thou canst not see my face: for there shall no man see me, and live.

But I want to tell you about the face I have never seen, which I long to see one day. It is the face of the Lord Jesus. One of my many favorite verses in the Bible was written by David, King of Israel.

One thing have I desired of the Lord, that will I seek after; that I may dwell in the house of the Lord all the days of my life, to behold the beauty of the Lord, and to inquire in his temple. (Exodus 33:18–23)

When we consider the face of Jesus, we see it from different aspects all mentioned in the scriptures.

A Disfigured Face

The face of Jesus was at one time disfigured as foretold by Isaiah. At His crucifixion, He was beaten until His face was unrecognizable. We read in Isaiah 50:6, "I gave my back to the smiters, and my cheeks to them that plucked off the hair: I hid not my face from shame and spitting."

Just as there were many who were appalled at him—His face was so disfigured beyond that of any man and his form marred beyond human likeness. (Isaiah 52:14 NIV)

Matthew and Mark recorded details of the cruelty meted out to Jesus. Matthew 27:29–30 reads,

> When they had platted a crown of thorns, they put it upon his head, and a reed in his right hand: and they bowed the knee before him, and mocked him, saying, Hail, King of the Jews! They spit upon him, and took the reed, and smote him on the head.

Mark 14:65 reads,

> And some began to spit on him, and to cover his face, and to buffet him and to say unto him, Prophesy! and the servants did strike him with the palms of their hands.

It is thought that the Scottish poet Robert Burns was the first person to coin the phrase "man's inhumanity to man," and we see plenty of it in the world today. Simon Weston CBE was horrifically burned when serving in the Falklands War in 1982. I will never forget his disfigured face; he was the most injured serviceman to survive when his ship was hit by bombs.

A Shining Face

When Jesus was transfigured on the mount, His face was shining brighter than the sun because it was a unique occasion. It was the glory of His person. It is the only time Jesus revealed His glory in this way while on the earth.

The word translated as "transfigured" has the same meaning

as metamorphosis, a change on the outside that comes from the inside. There was a change on the outside that came from within as He allowed His essential glory to shine forth (Hebrews 1:3). Matthew 17:2 (NIV) says, "He was transfigured before them. His face shone like the sun, and his clothes became as white as the light."

The light of God's glory shines out from the face of Jesus as we read in 2 Corinthians 4:6: "For God, who commanded the light to shine out of darkness, hath shined in our hearts, to give the light of the knowledge of the glory of God in the face of Jesus Christ."

A Majestic Face

Hebrews 2:9 reads, "But we see Jesus, who was made a little lower than the angels for the suffering of death, crowned with glory and honour; that he by the grace of God should taste death for every man."

A Lovely Face

> What is thy beloved more than another beloved? My beloved is white and ruddy, the chiefest among ten thousand. His head is as the finest gold, his locks are bushy, and black as a raven. His eyes are as the eyes of doves by the rivers of waters, washed with milk, and fitly set. His cheeks are as a bed of spices, as sweet flowers: his lips like lilies, dropping sweet smelling myrrh. (Song 5:9–13)

We surely must agree with the bride in the Song of Solomon as she looks upon the bridegroom, as we look upon Jesus, our Bridegroom: "He is the chiefest among ten thousand" (Song 5:10).

33

This Man

In the account of Jesus stilling the storm in Mark, the disciples said one to another, "What manner [kind] of man is this that even the wind and the sea obey Him?" (Mark 4:41). Through the ages, people have been asking the same question and have failed to recognize Jesus as the Son of God, who came into this world to pay the penalty for our sin.

Let me give some answers from the Bible that tell us about this Man.

He Is the Perfect Man

Luke records the verdict of one of the dying thieves on the cross: "*This man* hath done nothing amiss" (Luke 23:41).

Peter wrote,

> Knowing that you were ransomed from the futile ways inherited from your forefathers, not with perishable things such as silver or gold, but with the precious blood of Christ, like that of a lamb without blemish or spot. (1 Peter 1:18–19 ESV)

157

> Who did no sin, neither was guile found in his mouth. (1 Peter 2:22)

In Hebrews 4:15, we read "but [He] was in all points tempted like as we are, yet without sin." And in 7:26, we read, "Who is holy, harmless, undefiled, separate from sinners, and made higher than the heavens."

He Is the Condescending Man

The religious leaders in Jerusalem complained that *"This man* [Jesus] receives sinners and eats with them" (Luke 15:2 NKJV). Praise God! "He receives sinners!" Without Him, we would have no hope. What condescension!

When we think of Jesus coming into this world as a baby in a manger, our minds turn to Philippians 2: "Being in the form of God … made Himself of no reputation." Think of that. People spend their lives trying to make a reputation for themselves. Jesus, the Creator of all things, had a great reputation before He came into this world, but He condescended to such a degree as to make Himself of no reputation.

> For by him were all things created, that are in heaven, and that are in earth, visible and invisible, whether they be thrones, or dominions, or principalities, or powers: all things were created by him, and for him: And he is before all things, and by him all things consist.

> And he is the head of the body, the church: who is the beginning, the firstborn from the dead; that in all things he might have the pre-eminence. For

it pleased the Father that in him should all fulness dwell. (Colossians 1:16–19)

Despite His deity, He took the form of a servant and was made in the likeness of men. What condescension! But that was not enough, for we read that "being found in fashion as a man He humbled Himself." This man received sinners and ate with them; He washed His disciples' feet; He touched the leper. But even that was not sufficient. "He became obedient to [the extent of] death, even the death of the cross" (Philippians 2:8).

He Is the Forgiving Man

Be it known unto you therefore, men and brethren, that through *this man* is preached unto you the forgiveness of sins. (Acts 13:38)

The scribes accused Jesus of blasphemy because He forgave the sins of the palsied man let through the roof; they said, "Who can forgive sins, but God only" (Mark 2:7).

The scripture makes it quite clear that because of His death on the cross, we can have forgiveness of sins. What grace! Colossians 1:14 reads, "In whom we have redemption through his blood, even the forgiveness of sins."

He Is the Rejected Man

We will not have *this man* to reign over us. (Luke 19:14)

When we shall see him, there is no beauty that we should desire him. He is despised and rejected of men; a man of sorrows and acquainted with grief: and we hid as it were our faces from him; he was despised, and we esteemed him not. (Isaiah 53:2–3)

When they were gathered together, Pilate said unto them, Whom will ye that I release unto you? Barabbas, or Jesus which is called Christ? For he knew that for envy they had delivered him. But the chief priests and elders persuaded the multitude that they should ask Barabbas and destroy Jesus. The governor answered and said unto them, whether of the twain will ye that I release unto you? They said, Barabbas. (Matthew 27:17–21)

He Is the Exalted Man

But *this man*, after he had offered one sacrifice for sins for ever, sat down on the right hand of God. (Hebrews 10:12)

Peter and the other apostles responding to the high priest in Jerusalem answered and said,

The God of our fathers raised up Jesus, whom ye slew and hanged on a tree. Him hath God exalted with his right hand to be a Prince and a Saviour, for to give repentance to Israel, and forgiveness of sins. (Acts 5:30–31)

He Is the Glorified Man

For *this man* was counted worthy of more glory than Moses, inasmuch as he who hath builded the house hath more honour than the house. (Heb 3:3)

Jesus, the name He received when He was born, means Savior. John explained in the first chapter of his gospel that in the beginning, Jesus's name was "the Word."

Neither did he have a human body until He was born: "And the Word was made flesh, and dwelt among us, and we beheld his glory, the glory as of the only begotten of the Father, full of grace and truth" (John 1:14).

As the expected Messiah, Christ had other names; Isaiah 9:6 reads, "and his name shall be called Wonderful, Counsellor, The mighty God, The everlasting Father, The Prince of Peace."

He retained His human body when He was resurrected. In Luke 24:39–40, we have the record of His appearance in the upper room with His disciples when He told them,

> Behold my hands and my feet, that it is I myself: handle me, and see; for a spirit hath not flesh and bones, as ye see me have. And when he had thus spoken, he shewed them his hands and his feet.

It was the same body in which He ascended to heaven forty days after His resurrection, and it is that body which is glorified.

> And when he had spoken these things, while they beheld, he was taken up; and a cloud received him out of their sight. And while they looked steadfastly toward heaven as he went up, behold, two men stood by them in white apparel, which also said, Ye men of Galilee, why stand ye gazing up into heaven? this same Jesus, which is taken

> up from you into heaven, shall so come in like manner as ye have seen him go into heaven. (Acts 1:9–11)

As a result of His victory on the cross, He ascended into heaven with His earthly body, which has now been glorified.

> I have glorified thee on the earth: I have finished the work which thou gavest me to do. And now, O Father, glorify thou me with thine own self with the glory which I had with thee before the world was. (John 17:4–5)

34

Do Not Fret!

Reading: Psalm 37:1–8 (NKJV)

> Do not fret because of evildoers, nor be envious of
> the workers of iniquity, for they shall soon be cut
> down like the grass, and wither as the green herb.
> Trust in the Lord, and do good, dwell in the land,
> and feed on His faithfulness. Delight yourself also
> in the Lord, and He shall give you the desires of
> your heart. Commit your way to the Lord, trust
> also in Him, and He shall bring it to pass. He
> shall bring forth your righteousness as the light,
> and your justice as the noonday. Rest in the Lord
> and wait patiently for Him; Do not fret because
> of him who prospers in his way, because of the
> man who brings wicked schemes to pass. Cease
> from anger and forsake wrath; do not fret—it only
> causes harm.

In his psalm, David spoke about a conflict and then gave four
ways conflicts could be resolved. Each instruction is defined by

a word beginning with the letter *c*: confidence, contentment, commitment, and calmness.

But the background concerns conflict, but we need not be stressed and filled with anxiety if we put into practice the advice of King David. The first eight verses of Psalm 37 give us good advice on how to be free from fretting, and this is what we need in these times. I have highlighted the four things David mentioned in this psalm.

Confidence: Trust in the Lord

> Some trust in chariots, and some in horses: but we will remember [trust] the name of the Lord our God. (Psalm 20:7)

> Trust in the Lord with all thine heart; and lean not unto thine own understanding. (Proverbs 3:5)

Trust in God is the basis for all the blessings that flow from Him. Faith is to a Christian what a foundation is to a house; it gives confidence and assurance that God will be true to His Word: "The word of our God shall stand for ever" (Isaiah 40:8).

By trusting in God, we can dwell in the land. The Promised Land for the Israelites was not heaven; it was Canaan, and on numerous occasions, the people were urged to go in, conquer their enemies, and possess the land. For the believer, the land is still flowing with milk and honey, a land of many promises. Perhaps we do not take advantage of God's promises; perhaps we are not dwelling in the land. We can see it and read about it, but are we enjoying its wonderful promises?

Remember, God cannot break His promises; they are yea and amen. In 2 Peter 1:4, we read "Whereby are given unto us exceeding great and precious promises." By trusting in God, we can feed on His faithfulness and promises. One promise we should feed on is this: "He hath said, I will never leave thee, nor forsake thee" (Hebrews 13:5). Another is, "I go to prepare a place for you that where I am there ye may be also" (John 14:2–3), and there are hundreds more.

We should get to know His promises so we can feed on them; that will give us confidence and assurance, the antidote for stress and fretting. We have confidence in the Lord because we read in 1 Thessalonians 5:24, "Faithful is He that calleth you, who also will do it." And in Hebrews 10:23 we read, "Let us hold fast the profession of our faith without wavering; (for He is faithful that promised.)"

Contentment: Delight in the Lord

The word *delight* suggests complete satisfaction and contentment. The *Westminster Shorter Catechism* states that man's chief end is to glorify God and enjoy Him forever. Asaph, who wrote Psalm 73:25–26, said,

> Whom have I in heaven but thee? and there is none upon earth that I desire beside thee. My flesh and my heart faileth: but God is the strength of my heart, and my portion for ever.

David, the psalmist, wrote, "Delight thyself in the Lord" because He would give us the desires of our hearts. But this does not mean selfish desires. If we delight ourselves in the Lord, our desires will be right, and He will give them to us. The more we delight in Him, the closer we will be drawn to Him and the more our desires will fit in with His desires for us.

Since we came to know the Lord, we have a new life, new ambitions, and new desires of which Paul reminds the believers in Ephesians 2:3. Since we came to know Jesus as our Saviour, we had no interest or time for Him. He was a nobody. We saw no beauty in Him that we should want to love and serve Him.

But now things are different: "One thing have I desired of the Lord … that I may dwell in the house of the Lord [The Lord's presence] … to behold the beauty of the Lord" (Psalm 27).

In the Song of Songs, we read these words of the bride, His church, concerning the Bridegroom, Jesus.

> As an apple tree among the trees of the forest, so is my beloved among the young men. With great delight I sat in His shadow, and his fruit was sweet to my taste. He brought me to the banqueting house, and his banner over me was love. (Song 2:3–4 ESV)

Our delight should be in the Lord, who is the Rose of Sharon, the Lily of the Valley, and the Apple Tree under whose shadow we sit with great delight protected from the scorching heat of circumstances. That is true contentment.

Commitment: Commit Your Way unto the Lord

We prove our trust in the Lord when we commit the unknown pathways to Him knowing the truth of Proverbs 3:6: "In all thy ways, acknowledge Him, and He shall direct thy paths."

Psalm 37:5 reads, "Commit thy way unto the Lord." The Hebrew word for commitment is *gol*, which means rolling your way upon the Lord. The image is of our rolling off our shoulders burdens we are not able to bear on the shoulders of another, who is able to bear them (1 Peter 5:7; Psalm 55:22, 22:10). It means that our intentions, plans, and undertakings as explained in Proverbs 16:3 can be rolled as a burden upon the Lord.

Calmness—Rest in the Lord

Verse 7 reads, "Rest in the Lord and wait patiently for him: fret not thyself." Resting here means being quiet, silent, and still and not complaining. No need to fret or be envious but rather enter the calm that comes from being still in the Lord's presence.

Colloquially, we would say "Calm down." Don't be anxious when others around you seem to be prospering; be still before the Lord and wait patiently for Him for He will take care of your situation however difficult it is. Cast your burden on Him, who cares for you.

Jesus made this promise in Matthew 11:28: "Come unto me, all ye that labour and are heavy laden, and I will give you rest."

At the bedside of a sick patient, the doctor asked, "How are you today, sir?" to which the sick man replied, "My head is comfortably resting on three pillows—infinite power, infinite love, and infinite wisdom."

Ye have not because ye ask not. (James 4:2)

35

Paul's Prayer for the Ephesians

Reading: Ephesians 3:16–19

Paul prayed that the Ephesian believers would have strength, depth, understanding, and fullness. He prayed that they might have strength "that He would grant you, according to the riches of His glory, to be strengthened with might by His Spirit in the inner man."

In his prayer, he dealt with the spiritual condition of the inner man, not the material needs of the body. Sometimes, our prayers focus only on physical and material needs and fail to lay hold of the deeper needs of the soul, where the greatest needs are.

The New Testament mentions the inner man several times. In Romans 7:22 (NIV), Paul wrote, "For in my inner being I delight in God's law." In 2 Corinthians 4:16, Paul again referred to the need to be strong: "We faint not; but though our outward man perish, yet the inward man is renewed day by day."

We draw strength through the power of the Spirit, who enables us to live fruitful Christian lives, and Paul desires that power for his readers: "Ye shall receive power, when the Holy Spirit is come upon you" (Acts 1:8 ASV). This is one virtue we have for Christian living today.

The outer man is perishing, but the inner man is being renewed spiritually despite outward physical decay.

> Therefore, we do not lose heart, but though our outer man is decaying, yet our inner man is being renewed day by day. (2 Corinthians 4:16–18 NASB)

Having the Holy Spirit empower the inner man means that our new spiritual nature is controlled by God and we are developing our spiritual attributes and growing in the Word. Only when we yield to the Spirit and let Him control the inner man do we succeed in living to the glory of God. This means feeding the inner man on the Word of God.

Paul prayed that they might have depth in verse 17 (NASB) "that Christ may dwell in your hearts through faith; and that you, being rooted and grounded in love." He used three pictures to convey his idea of spiritual depth using three words: "dwell," "rooted," and "grounded."

To *dwell* somewhere means "to settle down and feel at home." Christ was already resident in the hearts of the Ephesians, and what Paul was praying for was a deeper experience between Christ and His people. He longed for Christ to settle down and feel at home in their hearts not in just a superficial relationship but in an ever-deepening fellowship. And that can be achieved only through faith. Paul used a similar expression when writing to the Colossians, also Gentiles, in 3:16: "Let the word of Christ dwell in you richly in all wisdom."

The word *rooted* takes us into the plant world. The tree must get its roots deep if it is to grow and have stability, and Christians must have spiritual roots that go deep into the love of God. Psalm 1:1–3 (RSV) offers a perfect description of this word.

> Blessed is the man who walks not in the counsel of the wicked, nor stands in the way of sinners, nor sits in the seat of scoffers; but his delight is in the law of the Lord, and on his law he meditates day and night. He is like a tree planted by streams of water, that yields its fruit in its season, and its leaf does not wither. In all that he does, he prospers.

Jeremiah 17:7–8 (NKJV) repeats the thought.

> Blessed is the man who trusts in the Lord, and whose hope is the Lord. For he shall be like a tree planted by the waters, which spreads out its roots by the river, and will not fear when heat comes; but its leaf will be green and will not be anxious in the year of drought, nor will cease from yielding fruit.

One of the most important questions Christians can ask themselves is, "From what do I draw nourishment and stability?" If there is to be power in the Christian life, there must be depth. The roots must go deeper and deeper into the love of Christ. Storms can reveal the strength of a tree's roots.

The word *grounded* takes us to the construction of a foundation for any building. Builders can take weeks laying out and pouring footings, the most important part of a building. If you don't go deep, you can't go high. Paul prayed that the believers might have a deeper experience of the love of Christ because only that could sustain them during the severe trials of life.

Paul prayed that they might have full understanding.

> That they may be able to comprehend with all the saints what is the width and length and depth and

height—to know the love of Christ which passes knowledge. (vv. 18–19a NKJV)

The words *comprehend* and *apprehend* stem from the Latin word *prehendere*, "to grasp." We say that a monkey has a prehensile tail, that is, a tail able to grasp branches and hold on. Thus, our word *comprehend* carries the idea of mentally grasping something while *apprehend* suggests laying hold of it for yourself. In other words, it is possible to understand something but not really make it your own.

Paul's concern was that we lay hold of the vastness of the love of God, but there is a paradox here. Paul wanted us to personally know the love of Christ "which surpasses knowledge." There are dimensions, but they cannot be measured. "The love of Christ which surpasses knowledge" parallels "the unsearchable riches of Christ" (Ephesians 3:8). We are so rich in Christ that our riches cannot be calculated.

No Christian should ever have to worry about having inadequate spiritual resources to meet the demands of life. Ask for spiritual strength and spiritual depth and God will enable you to apprehend, to get your hands on, all the resources of His love and grace. "I can do all things through Christ which strengtheneth me" (Philippians 4:13). And what is the result of all of this?

Fullness

That you may be filled up to all the fullness of God. (v. 19b NASU)

God wants us to experience His fullness, the filling of the Holy Spirit (Ephesians 5:18: "Be filled with the Spirit"), and the measure of our fullness is God Himself (Ephesians 4:11–15).

He gave some as apostles, and some as prophets, and some as evangelists, and some as pastors and teachers for the equipping of the saints to build up the body of Christ until we all attain unity of faith and knowledge of the Son of God.

But speaking the truth in love, we are to grow up in all aspects into Him who is the head, even Christ. (Eph 4:15 NASU).

We often use the wrong measurements to examine our spiritual lives. We like to measure ourselves against the weakest Christians we know and then boast, "I'm better than they are." Paul told us that the measure was Christ and that we should not boast about anything. When we have reached His fullness, we have reached the limit.

In one sense, the Christian is already "made full in Christ" because we read in Colossians 2:9–10, "For in him dwelleth all the fulness of the Godhead bodily. And ye are complete in him, which is the head of all principality and power." The word *complete* means "filled full."

Positionally, we are complete in Him, but practically, we enjoy only the infilling of the Holy Spirit through grace, which we lay hold of by faith. The resources are there. All we need do is accept and enjoy them.

36

Certainty

Reading: John 10:27–30

> My sheep hear my voice, and I know them, and
> they follow me: And I give unto them eternal life;
> and they shall never perish, neither shall any man
> pluck them out of my hand. My Father, which
> gave them me, is greater than all; and no man is
> able to pluck them out of my Father's hand. I and
> my Father are one.

The world faces a myriad of problems today including floods,
famine, hurricanes, and so much more. What's next? Are these
disasters due to our polluting the atmosphere, or are they due to
something like sunspots and are out of our control? There is a lot
of uncertainty, and the biggest uncertainty is when the pandemic
will end so we can get back to normalcy.

How about diet and health? Do we really know what foods
are good or bad for us? On the political front, are we heading
for another cold war with Russia? When will the war in Ukraine
come to an end? Does China have ambitions to conquer the

world? Is the civil war in Syria going to spill over into surrounding countries? Is Britain due for another terrorist attack? Are we getting out of the recession? There is so much uncertainty. Life is not guaranteed. Even the philosophers will agree that death is certain, and that life insurance does not insure us against death. How about life after death? Can we be certain where we will spend eternity?

Psalm 31:15 reads, "My times are in God's hand," but for the Christian, even death is not certain because the Lord is coming to catch up all believers. It is certain to happen; the only uncertainty is when.

However, there is no need for uncertainty about where you will spend eternity. The wonderful thing about the Christian faith is that it does give certainty. You can be sure about your eternal future because it is based on God's Word and the words of Jesus Christ. There are numerous promises of eternal life in the Bible, but here is one in John 6:47 (NKJV): "Most assuredly, I say to you, he who believes in Me has everlasting life." Not "might have," not "will have," but present tense "has right now" eternal life.

In the above reading from John 10:27–30 Jesus said concerning His followers,

> I give unto them eternal life; and they shall never perish, neither shall any man pluck them out of my hand. My Father, which gave them me, is greater than all; and no man is able to pluck them out of my Father's hand.

Christians can have confidence in the promises of the Bible. Unfortunately, there are many today who think trusting in the Lord for salvation is too easy. Jesus said that childlike faith was needed.

One day some parents brought their children to Jesus so he could touch and bless them. But the disciples scolded the parents for bothering him. When Jesus saw what was happening, he was angry with his disciples. He said to them, Let the children come to me. Don't stop them! For the Kingdom of God belongs to those who are like these children. I tell you the truth, anyone who doesn't receive the Kingdom of God like a child will never enter it. (Mark 10:13–16 NLT)

Around 900 BC, when Naaman, the captain of the king of Syria's army, found that he had leprosy, he was willing to pay a considerable sum to the king of Israel to be cured: "ten talents of silver, and six thousand pieces of gold, and ten changes of raiment" (2 Kings 5:5). But that did not provide the answer.

When he met with Elisha, the man of God, he was expecting Elisha to perform some showy spectacle to heal him, but no spectacular show was the answer either. Elisha told him all he needed to do was to wash seven times in the Jordan River; what could have been simpler? But he wanted to wash in a river of his own choice; he thought he knew better than God's prophet. However, his servants persuaded him to do what Elisha told him.

The reason I am quoting from the account of Naaman (2 Kings 5) is that it was a little girl's faith that led Naaman to be healed.

And the Syrians had gone out by companies and had brought away captive out of the land of Israel a little maid; and she waited on Naaman's wife. And she said unto her mistress, Would God my lord were with the prophet that is in Samaria! for he would recover him of his leprosy. (2 Kings 5:2–3)

You will remember that before He went to the cross, Jesus said to His disciples,

> Let not your heart be troubled … In my Father's house are many mansions. If it were not so I would have told you. I go to prepare a place for you. (John 14:1–2)

We can have confidence if we rest on the unfailing promises of God. Paul, who was full of confidence about his relationship with God, wrote in 2 Timothy 1:12 (TLB), "I know the one in whom I trust, and I am sure that he is able to safely guard all that I have given him until the day of his return."

There are of course other certainties that true believers in Christ possess— forgiveness of sins and adoption into the family of God—but most wonderfully, God's love for them. They all stem from the one great fact that Jesus died for our sins. We must remember that God keeps His promises.

> God is not a man, that he should lie; neither the son of man, that he should repent: hath he said, and shall he not do it? or hath he spoken, and shall he not make it good? (Numbers 23:19)

One of the certainties in life is mentioned in 1 Timothy 6:6–8.

> But godliness with contentment is great gain. For we brought nothing into this world, and it is certain we can carry nothing out. And having food and raiment let us be therewith content.

If we are earthly minded, we shall put our priority on seeking to amass corruptible and perishable assets instead of investing in heavenly things. Jesus said life was more than meat and the body more than raiment. He also said,

> Lay not up for yourselves treasures upon earth, where moth and rust doth corrupt, and where thieves break through and steal: But lay up for yourselves treasures in heaven, where neither moth nor rust doth corrupt, and where thieves do not break through nor steal: For where your treasure is, there will your heart be also.

> No man can serve two masters: for either he will hate the one and love the other; or else he will hold to the one and despise the other. Ye cannot serve God and mammon. Therefore, I say unto you, take no thought for your life, what ye shall eat, or what ye shall drink; nor yet for your body, what ye shall put on. Is not the life more than meat, and the body than raiment?

> Behold the fowls of the air: for they sow not, neither do they reap, nor gather into barns; yet your heavenly Father feedeth them. Are ye not much better than they? Which of you by taking thought can add one cubit unto his stature? And why take ye thought for raiment? Consider the lilies of the field, how they grow; they toil not, neither do they spin:

> And yet I say unto you, that even Solomon in all his glory was not arrayed like one of these. Wherefore, if God so clothe the grass of the field, which today is, and tomorrow is cast into the oven,

shall he not much more clothe you, O ye of little faith?

Therefore, take no thought, saying, what shall we eat? or, what shall we drink? or, wherewithal shall we be clothed? (For after all these things do the Gentiles seek:) for your heavenly Father knoweth that ye have need of all these things. But seek ye first the kingdom of God, and his righteousness; and all these things shall be added unto you. (Matthew 6:19–33)

37

Bundle of Life

"Bundle of life" is an intriguing expression in 1 Samuel 25:29. As David was fleeing his enemy, Saul, Abigail provided food for him and his men because they were famished. She told David,

> Yet a man has risen to pursue you and seek your life, but the life of my lord shall be bound in the bundle of life with the Lord your God. (1 Samuel 25:29 NKJV)

In those primitive days, they did not have elaborate means of securing anything safely. When they shifted their tents to new pastures, anything of special value would simply be bound up in a bundle that the husband or wife would look after on the journey.

It is an amazing and a beautiful thought that our lives could be bound up with God's life, and yet this is a fact as far as believers in the Lord Jesus are concerned. Our lives are intertwined in such a way that they are fastened to each other. Such thoughts are beyond our understanding.

We read in 2 Corinthians 5:19 that God was in Christ, that Christ was in the bosom of the Father (John 1:18), that believers are in Christ (numerous scriptures), and that Christ is in believers (Colossians 1:27; Galatians 2:20). We also know that the Holy Spirit dwells in us. What a bundle of life!

The blessings of being bound up in the life of God are numerous. The first word that comes to my mind is *security*. Jesus told the unbelieving Jews gathered around Him concerning His sheep in John 10:28–30,

> I give unto them eternal life; and they shall never perish, neither shall any man pluck them out of my hand. My Father, which gave them me, is greater than all; and no man is able to pluck them out of my Father's hand. I and my Father are one.

Another word that comes to mind is *separation* because believers can be sure nothing can separate them from God's love. We are bound up in the bundle of life with God. Romans 8:35–39 states,

> Who shall separate us from the love of Christ? shall tribulation, or distress, or persecution, or famine, or nakedness, or peril, or sword? I am persuaded that neither death, nor life, nor angels, nor principalities, nor powers, nor things present, nor things to come, nor height, nor depth, nor any other creature [created thing], shall be able to separate us from the love of God which is in Christ Jesus our Lord.

Another blessing that comes from being bound in the bundle of life with God is sanctification—being set apart for a purpose. To sanctify someone or something is to set that person or thing apart for the use intended by its designer. A pen is sanctified when it is used to write. Spectacles are sanctified when used to improve eyesight. In the biblical sense, things are sanctified when they are used for the purpose God intended. Human beings are sanctified when they are saved.

> So that they may receive forgiveness for their sins and God's inheritance along with all people everywhere whose sins are cleansed away, who are set apart by faith in me. (Acts 26:18 TLB)

The Holy Spirit is the agent in sanctification. Just think of some of the things it means to have the Spirit of God living in us. I have drawn some thoughts from Romans 8 concerning the doctrine of the indwelling Holy Spirit. The believer is the dwelling place of God's Holy Spirit. Romans 8:9 (NKJV) reads, "But you are not in the flesh but in the Spirit, if indeed the Spirit of God dwells in you. Now if anyone does not have the Spirit of Christ, he is not His."

When we were saved, we were set apart to and for God. There is also, however, the sense that our sanctification may describe our present state. In other words, we should ask ourselves, "Are we living in a way that it can be said that we are set apart to God?"

We have a new life. We are not bound by the old nature; we are now free from it. Therefore, we should not live according to the old nature but according to the Spirit. Life in Christ through the Spirit offers us so many new things. Here are a few.

We have new desires.

> Those who live according to the sinful nature have their minds set on what that nature desires; but those who live in accordance with the Spirit have their minds set on what the Spirit desires. (Romans 8:5 NIV)

Have you noticed that your desires were changed since you trusted the Lord, or are you still hankering after the things of the old life?

We have new thinking.

> And be not conformed to this world: but be ye transformed by the renewing of your mind, that ye may prove what is that good, and acceptable, and perfect, will of God. (Romans 12:2)

> Set your minds on things above, not on earthly things. Put to death, therefore, whatever belongs to your earthly nature. (Colossians 3:1–5 NIV)

We have a new prospect.

> We are predestined to be conformed to the image [likeness] of His Son, that He might be the firstborn among many brothers. (Romans 8:29 ESV)

What a bundle of life! Thank you, Lord.

38

Were You There?

I looked on the internet to see who wrote the song "Were You There?" Does anyone know who wrote that lovely hymn? No. It is anonymous. Did you know it is a Negro spiritual from the mid-1700s in the southern states of America sung by African American slaves?

When I read about this, I decided to learn a bit about the slaves and the slave masters of the past especially in the US. But first, let us read some passages in the Bible.

> Don't you realize that you become the slave of whatever you choose to obey? You can be a slave to sin, which leads to death, or you can choose to obey God, which leads to a right relationship with God. (Romans 6:16–18 NLT)

> Jesus said to the people who believed on him, you are truly my disciples if you remain faithful to my teachings. And you will know the truth, and the truth will set you free. We have never been slaves to anyone. What do you mean, you

> will be set free? Jesus replied, I tell you the truth,
> everyone who sins is a slave of sin. A slave is not a
> permanent member of the family, but a son is part
> of the family forever. So, if the Son sets you free,
> you are truly free. (John 8:31–36 NLT)

The slaves who sang the spirituals, sometimes called slave songs, were mostly Africans who had been sold by the slave traders and brought over to America. It is reckoned that about twelve million slaves arrived in America between the sixteenth and nineteenth centuries. Most ended up in Brazil, but about one million were sold to plantation owners in the southern states. They were treated as chattel, property that could be bought and sold.

It is almost impossible for us to appreciate the suffering of the slaves working from sunrise to sunset on plantations. They were beaten, their wives were abused, and their children were often separated from their parents. Deaths were commonplace; their owners considered their lives worthless. It was nothing for a slave to be found hanged.

Very strangely, it was only recently that I listened on Radio 4 to a woman who was a descendant of a slave; she spoke about a slave song called "Strange Fruit Hanging from the Poplar Tree." They were not allowed freedom to set up their own churches and were forbidden to read the Bible. And they were deliberately kept illiterate. They were only allowed to go to church with their masters and mistresses, and that is where they learned about Moses and the children of Israel. In their misery, they learned to sing songs with a meaning and very often based on Bible stories. And they soon developed songs that also carried secret messages. Only the slaves knew their meaning. Coded messages were often spread around about rebellions and escapes. It was during the Great Awakening (1730–1750) that English evangelist George Whitefield preached the gospel to these slaves, and many were saved.

They would sing around the campfires about the freedom they longed for, about the children of Israel who were released by Moses from their slavery in Egypt. The best future they could hope for was to be in heaven with Jesus when their pain and misery ended. The river Jordan was the code word for death. "Ol' man river" refers to death, which relentlessly rolls on.

They sang these plantation songs to encourage each other. You can easily interpret the meanings behinds some of the words. "Michael, Row the Boat Ashore," "Swing Low, Sweet Chariot, coming for to Carry Me Home," "Roll, Jordan, Roll," "Deep River, My Home Is over Jordan." Sometimes, the coded meanings made fun of their masters though their masters didn't realize it. Words like *Satan* referred to slave masters.

Slaves could easily identify in a powerful way with the suffering of Christ and how He was beaten and led as a lamb to the slaughter. They could identify with His suffering and abuse at the hands of Jews and Romans. Why did He allow Himself to be nailed to a cross? He could have called heavenly hosts of angels to save Him, but He died to save us all.

In a sense, we are all slaves. We are under the control of a master. Jesus said,

> No man can serve two masters: for either he will hate the one and love the other; or else he will hold to the one and despise the other. Ye cannot serve God and mammon. (Matthew 6:24)

As our scripture reading in John 8:34 (NLT) stated,

> I tell you the truth, everyone who sins is a slave of sin. A slave is not a permanent member of the family, but a son is part of the family forever. So, if the Son sets you free, you are truly free.

By singing the song "Were You There When They Crucified My Lord?" they were identifying themselves with the suffering Savior and appreciating how much Jesus suffered. They knew Jesus had triumphed over death and had gained the victory for He rose from the grave.

The apostle Paul knew what slavery to sin was.

> The trouble is with me, for I am all too human, a slave to sin. I don't really understand myself, for I want to do what is right, but I don't do it. Instead, I do what I hate. But if I know that what I am doing is wrong, this shows that I agree that the law is good. So, I am not the one doing wrong; it is sin living in me that does it.

> And I know that nothing good lives in me, that is, in my sinful nature. I want to do what is right, but I can't. I want to do what is good, but I don't. I don't want to do what is wrong, but I do it anyway. I have discovered this principle of life—that when I want to do what is right, I inevitably do what is wrong. I love God's law with all my heart.

> But there is another power within me that is at war with my mind. This power makes me a slave to the sin that is still within me. Oh, what a miserable person I am! Who will free me from this life that is dominated by sin and death? Thank God! The answer is in Jesus Christ our Lord. (Romans 7:14–25 NLT)

For over 3,500 years, Jews did not forget the time when their people were slaves in Egypt. Moses was instrumental in carrying out God's plan to rescue His people from their oppressors. We have this account in Exodus 3:7–8.

> And the Lord said, I have surely seen the affliction of my people which are in Egypt and have heard their cry by reason of their taskmasters; for I know their sorrows; and I am come down to deliver them out of the hand of the Egyptians, and to bring them up out of that land unto a good land and a large, unto a land flowing with milk and honey.

The Jews were to kill a lamb and sprinkle its blood on the doorposts and lintels of their homes so that when the destroying angel of the Lord passed over Egypt, their firstborn sons would be spared. That caused their Egyptian taskmasters to rapidly free the Israelites under the leadership of Moses. And ever since then, Jews have remembered their deliverance by celebrating Passover.

We Christians remember that the blood of the Lamb of God was shed to redeem us. The Lord Jesus asked us to remember Him in the breaking of bread, communion, as often as we can until He comes to rapture His children home.

> Surely, I come quickly. Amen. Even so, come, Lord Jesus. (Revelation 22:20–21)

39

Gathered to the Lord

Reading: Matthew 18:20

> Where two or three are gathered together in My name there I am in the midst of them.

This verse brings three thoughts to my mind: a special gathering, a special presence, and a special focus.

A Special Gathering

This verse is relevant to all our church services; we have the necessary quorum (two or three) when we gather. In 1 Corinthians 11:20, Paul referred to the breaking of bread service as a coming together: "When you come together [to break bread]." In Acts 20:7, Luke wrote, "On the first day of the week when the disciples came together to break bread ..."

God wants His saints to be gathered to Him. We read in Psalm 50:5, "Gather my saints together unto Me those that have made a covenant with Me by sacrifice." I like the word *together* because it implies a close relationship. In Psalm 133:1 we read, "Behold, how good and how pleasant it is for brethren to dwell together in unity."

When we get to heaven, we shall be together for a long time.

> But God, who is rich in mercy, for his great love wherewith he loved us, even when we were dead in sins, hath quickened us together with Christ, (by grace ye are saved). And hath raised us up together and made us sit together in heavenly places in Christ Jesus. (Ephesians 2:4–6)

The word *together* occurs three times in these three verses: alive together, raised together, and sit together. There is a special meaning to being gathered. It is similar to the phrase "with one accord" used in Acts to describe how the early believers met in their church.

> They continued with one accord in prayer. (Acts 1:14)

> They lifted up their voice to God with one accord. (Acts 4:24)

> They continued daily with one accord in the temple. (Acts 2:46)

> When the Day of Pentecost was fully come, they were all with one accord in one place. (Acts 2:1)

> Fulfil ye my joy that ye be like-minded, having the same love, being of one accord of one mind. (Philippians 2:2)

Being gathered implies a closeness, a oneness with a common purpose. This is how Paul spoke of the coming together to break bread in 1 Corinthians 10:17: "We, being many are one bread, and one body; for we are all partakers of that one bread." The idea is fellowship. Thus, words such as communion, partakers, and fellowship used in chapter 10 describe gathering to break bread, and this fellowship is not only with each other but with the Lord Himself.

This idea brings with it a responsibility for each of us to see that there is nothing in us that spoils this togetherness—not unkind thoughts, grudges, or jealousy. Paul stated this clearly in 1 Corinthians 11:27–28, which warns against taking the bread and wine unworthily and instructs us to examine ourselves before taking the emblems.

A Special Presence

Jesus promised that where two or three were gathered in His name—that is, with His authority and upholding His honor and dignity—He would be present. Can we grasp that awesome fact?

In June 1520, Henry VIII and King Francis of France met near Calais at the Field of Cloth of Gold in an attempt to strengthen the bond between the two countries. Each king tried to outshine the other with dazzling tents and clothes, grand feasts, music, jousting, and games. The tents and the costumes included such quantities of cloth of gold that the site of the meeting was named after it. These men were earthly kings trying to show off their glory, to be the center of attraction, but we have the presence of the King of Kings. None with Him can compare.

Notice that Jesus did not say, "I will be in the midst of them." He said, "I am in the midst of them." We know that His presence is a divine presence; it demands our awe and due reverence.

A Special Focus

The focal point of our church gatherings is not a doctrine, or the observance of some ritual, or the practice of some tradition. The focal point is a person—Christ, and in particular His sacrifice for us. I say this because when He comes among us by His Holy Spirit, He is in our midst. He does not take a back seat so that He won't be noticed. When He instituted this supper, He said, "This do in remembrance of Me" (Luke 22:19).

Jesus is the object of our gathering and the one we come to worship. God intends as we read in Colossians "that in all things Christ should have the pre-eminence."

Here are some other occasions when Jesus was in the midst.

- As a boy of twelve, He was in the midst as a teacher of the religious scholars.
- On the cross, He was crucified with two thieves and was in their midst as the Savior.
- On the resurrection day, He stood in the midst in the upper room as the risen Lord.
- In Revelation 5, we see the Lord in the midst of the throne as the worthy Lamb.
- In Revelation 2, we see Him walking in the midst of the golden lampstands, the churches, as the head of the church.
- And here in Matthew 18:20, we see Jesus in the midst as the divine presence.

May we focus our spiritual eyes and our minds on Him each time we gather in church to give Him the praise due Him and as we remember we are in His presence.

40

Wonderful Grace

Justice is getting what you deserve. Mercy is not getting what you deserve. And grace is getting what you do not deserve.

We are living in the Day of Grace, by which we mean that God's dealings with humankind are governed by grace. He is offering us things we do not deserve. In Titus 2:11–14, Paul explained what God's grace had produced in the child of God. I have described it under four headings.

- What grace has brought
- What grace has taught
- What grace has wrought
- What grace has sought

For the grace of God that *bringeth* salvation hath appeared to all men, *teaching* us that, denying ungodliness and worldly lusts, we should live soberly, righteously, and godly, in this present world; *looking for that blessed hope*, and the glorious appearing of the great God and our Saviour Jesus Christ, who gave himself for us, that he might redeem us from all iniquity, and purify unto himself a *peculiar people*, zealous of good works. (Emphasis added)

What Grace Has Brought

We are saved only by God's amazing grace. Ephesians 2:8–9 reads, "For by grace are ye saved through faith; and that not of yourselves: it is the gift of God; not of works, lest any man should boast." Paul said, "The grace of God brings salvation."

What Grace Has Taught

Paul mentions two categories to describe what grace has taught—the negative and the positive. Negatively, Paul was saying that grace had taught us to deny ungodliness and worldly lusts. Positively, he was saying that grace was teaching us to live sober, righteous, and godly lives; we should live for God, not for ourselves.

What Grace Has Wrought

This refers to what grace is producing in our lives—a longing for "that blessed hope and glorious appearing of the great God, and our Saviour Jesus Christ."

> Beloved, now are we the sons of God, and it doth not yet appear what we shall be: but we know that, when he shall appear, we shall be like him; for we shall see him as he is. And every man that hath this hope in him purifieth himself, even as he is pure. (1 John 3:2–3)

What Grace Has Sought

The result of being saved by grace is the redemption of a peculiar people zealous of good works. Here, the true meaning of the word *peculiar* is "a people for His own possession"; it does not mean "odd" or "strange."

> Which in time past were not a people but are now
> the people of God: which had not obtained mercy,
> but now have obtained mercy. (1 Peter 2:10)

The story of Mephibosheth in 2 Samuel 9:1–13 is a story of grace (loving-kindness). His grandfather was King Saul, the first king of Israel. He was attractive, and he showed prowess as a military leader. Mephibosheth's father was Jonathan, the oldest son of King Saul. He was the commander of a thousand men and was renowned for his successful battles against the Philistines and particularly the battle at Michmash, when Israel successfully overthrew its oppressors. Perhaps the best-known fact about Jonathan was his friendship with David.

Mephibosheth was only five when his father and grandfather died on Mount Gilboa in the Battle of Jezreel. When the child's nurse heard the outcome of the battle, she feared for Mephibosheth's life and fled for his protection. "He fell and became lame," and for the rest of his life, he was crippled.

We can summarize Mephibosheth's family background in this way.

A Doomed Family

Saul wasted his time trying to kill David; 2 Samuel 3:1 tells us that there was war between the house of Saul and the house of David. David was getting stronger while Saul was getting weaker.

When David heard that Jonathan and some of his brothers had been killed at the battle of Jezreel and that Saul had committed suicide, he mourned, fasted, and grieved.

A Disgraced Family

King Saul began his reign with great promise but ended it in shame. He had a rebellious nature. When God told him to destroy the Amalekites and their belongings, he defeated the army but kept some of the spoils. His disobedience showed that he could not be trusted to obey God. Although he was allowed to remain king for the rest of his life, the Spirit of the Lord had departed from him. David was anointed king in his place.

A Destitute Family

Because Mephibosheth was a descendant of Saul, he too was doomed to die, and his execution might have been imminent, so he moved to a distant land presumably for safety. The Bible tells us that he was living in a place called Lodebar, which means "no pasture." It was in the house of Machir, which means "sold." Mephibosheth was living in a place of poverty and want. He was destitute.

A Disabled Family

Mephibosheth was a cripple. He had been dropped by his nurse when he was five and was lame (2 Samuel 4:4) and could not work. He had inherited nothing but poverty and death. He was in a desperate situation.

A *Desired Family*

But how wonderful! Things changed for the better. After David heard of the deaths of Saul and Jonathan, he wanted to show kindness to anyone left in Saul's family, so he reached out to Mephibosheth because of the love he had for Jonathan. This disgraced, doomed, destitute, and disabled family had become a desired family.

King David asked Ziba, his servant,

> Is there not yet any of the house of Saul, that I
> may shew the kindness of God unto him? And
> Ziba said unto the king, Jonathan hath yet a son,
> which is lame on his feet. (2 Sam 9:3)

David sent for Mephibosheth and brought him into his palace to sit at the king's table and to be treated as one of the king's sons. This is a picture of what God has done for us, a disgraced, doomed, destitute, and disabled family. He proved His love for us when He sent Jesus to die on the cross for our sins. We could not buy or work our way to God. Just like Mephibosheth, we were lame, helpless, and hopeless before God, who showed us His loving-kindness. Let us look at the gracious act of David and how Mephibosheth became David's friend.

David sought him. Just like Jesus, the Good Shepherd sought for the lost sheep. (Luke 15). God sent Jesus into the world to save sinners. Luke 19:10 reads, "For the Son of man is come to seek and to save that which was lost."

He sent for Him. He could have refused to come to David's palace. David sent his servant to fetch Mephibosheth. This was the attitude of the Savior. He constantly asked people to come to Him never turning them away.

Do you want rest? Come to Jesus. Jesus said,

Come unto me, all ye that labour and are heavy
laden, and I will give you rest. Take my yoke upon
you and learn of me; for I am meek and lowly
in heart: and ye shall find rest unto your souls.
(Matthew 11:28–29)

As I said, Mephibosheth did not have to accept King David's
invitation to the palace. He had a free will. But for a destitute
and lame man living in the wilderness, it made sense for him to
accept the king's invitation. Indeed, it could have been regarded
as a snub to the king had he not accepted such a wonderful offer.
King David spoke to him.

Fear not: for I will surely shew thee kindness for
Jonathan thy father's sake and will restore thee
all the land of Saul thy father; and thou shalt eat
bread at my table continually. (2 Samuel 9:7)

And Mephibosheth's response was that he bowed himself and
confessed his unworthiness.

What is thy servant, that thou shouldest look upon
such a dead dog as I am? (2 Samuel 9:8)

He spared him—a dead dog. "Mephibosheth shall eat bread
always at my table." This reminds us of what Paul wrote in Romans
8:32, that God "spared not His own Son, but delivered Him up [to
the cross] for us all, how shall He not with Him also freely give
us all things?"

As the apple tree among the trees of the wood, so is
my beloved among the sons. I sat down under his

Come, Let Us Reason

41

Reading: Isaiah 1:18

> Come now, and let us reason together, saith the Lord: though your sins be as scarlet, they shall be as white as snow.

It is a good thing to remind ourselves of the wonder of the gospel message and of what it cost the Lord to provide salvation for us lost sinners. This text from Isaiah 1:18 is an invitation to the world from God Himself.

- He says come now—It is a summons.
- Let us reason together—It is a sensible invitation.
- Says the Lord—It is a serious invitation from God Himself.
- Though your sins are like scarlet, they shall be white as snow—It is a sin-cleansing invitation.

We like receiving invitations especially to weddings or celebrations; they make us feel special and show that we have friends who value our company. A man invites a woman out on a date; a businessman invites a client out for lunch; a housewife invites her neighbor for coffee.

God has issued invitations to each of us. He is offering to forgive our sins if we are willing to come to Him. You would think that God, who hates sin, would be the last person to invite us to come to Him. Would He not be repelled by the stain of sin on our lives? Well, the good news of the Christian gospel is that although God hates sin, He loves the sinner—you and me. That's why He says, "Come," not "Go away."

The UK is ranked as one of the richest countries in the world, and yet there are more than 280,000 homeless people in England. It leads to people sleeping rough in the streets in all weather conditions. It is a blight on our nation. They sleep in all sorts of places—under bridges, in town centers, and in more-remote places. Imagine that you were down and out sleeping rough under a hedge in the countryside. You have just settled into your sleeping bag, and you are wondering where your next day's food will come from. Just as you are dozing off, you see the light of a torch. Someone is searching for something or somebody and shouts, "Hey Joe! Here's someone sleeping under this hedge!" You take fright and wonder what will happen next: *Am I going to be arrested? Or attacked?* You then see a face in the torchlight and hear that the lord of the manor is holding a feast in his mansion down the road tonight and is inviting you it.

Everything is ready for the feast, and you are invited to come. But you say, "I haven't any decent clothes. In fact, what I am wearing are rags. Furthermore, I have no money. I cannot pay for anything." The man with the torch says, "Don't worry about that. The master says you can come just as you are. He will fit you up with some nice clothes. And the feast is free. All you need to do is to accept the invitation."

The truth is that Jesus is saying, "Come," to all sinners just as they are because He can forgive their sins and make them clean and fit in the sight of God. Just like the lord of the manor, Jesus has paid the bill so that we can enjoy a menu of joy, peace, hope, love, faith, and many other blessings. He was qualified to bear God's judgment for our sins because He was the sinless Son of God.

> Then said he unto him, A certain man made a great supper, and bade many: and sent his servant at supper time to say to them that were bidden, come; for all things are now ready. And they all with one consent began to make excuse. The first said unto him, I have bought a piece of ground, and I must needs go and see it: I pray thee have me excused. And another said, I have bought five yoke of oxen, and I go to prove them: I pray thee have me excused. And another said, I have married a wife, and therefore I cannot come.
>
> So that servant came and shewed his lord these things. Then the master of the house being angry said to his servant, go out quickly into the streets and lanes of the city, and bring in hither the poor, and the maimed, and the halt, and the blind. And the servant said, Lord, it is done as thou hast commanded, and yet there is room. And the lord said unto the servant, go out into the highways and hedges, and compel them to come in, that my house may be filled. (Luke 14:16–23)

When He was on the cross, Jesus cried out, "It is finished!" That did not mean that Jesus was finished but that the work He had come to do was completed. The bill was paid. Sinners could be forgiven and receive eternal life and have new lives by being born again.

I said earlier that it is a serious invitation from God, and there are serious consequences if His invitation is ignored or refused.

If I were to say that it was quite hard for God to forgive you, what would you think? I believe I know what would happen. You would misunderstand me, and it would not be your fault. My words might seem to imply a reluctance on God's part as though I meant that God could hardly bring Himself to pardon you or that His pardon if and when it came would be half-hearted or grudging. But I would not mean that at all.

Nevertheless, it was not easy for God to pay for our salvation; indeed, it was a very hard and costly price to pay. God does not save sinners reluctantly, but He does so at great cost. It is not hard for God to bring Himself to rescue men, but the way He chose to do it brought enormous pain and sorrow on Christ Jesus. That is the sense in which it was hard.

The crux of the Christian faith is that God's Son died on a cross. Jesus was not born in royal splendor; He did not spend His days in a life of ease. Far from it! But what is all that compared to the way His life on earth ended? He was mocked and despised by men for whom He prayed, and at the cross, He was forsaken by His Father. And yet this terrific sight reveals the heart of our message: if you want forgiveness, you will find it in His death. You will find it at the cross or not at all. His death (and ultimate resurrection) pardons the penitent sinner.

The Bible, God's message to humankind, contains many instances when God and Jesus Christ said, "Come." Isaiah 1:18 is an open invitation to come to Him, a summons to come into His presence and discuss our problems and the failures in our lives. The good news is that if we come to Him, He will make sure we have done the right thing in coming to Him because He says it is sensible to do so; let us reason together. He wants you and me to consider our lives, and He has a reasonable proposition to make, which will be life changing.

42

Blindness

What does the Bible have to say about blindness? Jesus's agenda was stated in Luke 4:16–19.

> He came to Nazareth, where He had been brought up: and, as His custom was, He went into the synagogue on the sabbath day, and stood up for to read. And there was delivered unto him the book of the prophet Esaias.

> And when he had opened the book, he found the place where it was written, The Spirit of the Lord is upon me, because he hath anointed me to preach the gospel to the poor; he hath sent me to heal the brokenhearted, to preach deliverance to the captives, and recovering of sight to the blind, to set at liberty them that are bruised, to preach the acceptable year of the Lord.

Jesus gave sight to the physically blind such as Bartimaeus and gave sight to the spiritually blind as explained by Paul when he wrote to the Corinthians.

> The god of this world hath blinded the minds of them which believe not, lest the light of the glorious gospel of Christ, who is the image of God, should shine unto them. (2 Corinthians 4:4)

We know that God sometimes takes one gift and gives another. We know that if one of our senses is impaired, we are compensated by an improvement in other senses. For example, it is said that a blind man develops more-sensitive hearing. There are many Christians who have proven this is true. John Newton apparently was blind in later life, and the prolific hymn writer Fanny Crosby, who lived almost throughout the nineteenth century and who wrote more than seven thousand hymns, became blind from the age of six weeks. A doctor had given her the wrong treatment for an eye condition. Some of her hymns are still popular today, such as "Blessed Assurance Jesus Is Mine," "Safe in the Arms of Jesus," "I Am Thine, O Lord," and many others.

I attend a virtual prayer meeting with my wife every Thursday morning, and one of those who attends calls himself Merthyr Mark because he comes from the town of Merthyr in the Welsh valleys. His beautiful prayers bring tears to my eyes.

The strange thing about Merthyr Mark is that he always prays with his eyes wide open looking upward. We were told that Mark was blind, but I think it is certain his vision of the Savior is clear and focused. What an inspiration he is to us!

Jesus restored sight to blind Bartimaeus (see Mark 10). However, there was another blind man healed by Jesus. (John 9).

> And as Jesus passed by, he saw a man which was blind from his birth, and his disciples asked him, saying, Master, who did sin, this man, or his

parents, that he was born blind? Jesus answered, neither hath this man sinned, nor his parents: but that the works of God should be made manifest in him. As long as I am in the world, I am the light of the world.

When he had thus spoken, he spat on the ground, and made clay of the spittle, and he anointed the eyes of the blind man with the clay, and said unto him, Go, wash in the pool of Siloam, (which is by interpretation, Sent.) He went his way therefore, and washed, and came seeing.

From then on there was confusion among the neighbours as to whether this was the man who was born blind.

Therefore, said they unto him, how were thine eyes opened? He answered and said, A man that is called Jesus made clay, and anointed mine eyes, and said unto me, go to the pool of Siloam, and wash; and I went and washed, and I received sight.

They were obviously reluctant to believe that Jesus had healed him. They questioned him as to where Jesus was, and he said he did not know. Therefore, they brought him to the pharisees and told them the story. It happened to be the Sabbath day that Jesus had taken clay to place on the man's blind eyes. Some of the Pharisees said of Jesus, this man is not of God because "he keepeth not the sabbath day." The discussion carried on, now questioning who Jesus was, and involving the once blind man's parents.

> The healed man said of Jesus, "whether he be a
> sinner or no, I know not: one thing I know is, that
> whereas I was blind, now I see." (John 9:1–7)

I had another friend, Peter, who was blind. We first met over fifty years ago in Birmingham in the West Midlands of the UK. I used to sing with a gospel male quartet, and he would accompany us on the piano. He was also a pastor at a church. We lost touch after my family moved to the North Midlands. He was such a talented pianist that he could play any hymn tune and in any style, whether Mozart, Chopin, Brahms, Bach, or any other composer.

When I retired from work, we moved back to South Wales, where my wife and I had been born and brought up. Wales is known as the Land of Song. I used to sing solos and duets with my brother in my Sunday school days from the age of ten. Now that we had returned to South Wales, I joined the South Wales Gospel Male Voice Choir. We used to have annual festivals of praise in Swansea in a grand concert hall called the Brangwyn Hall.

At one festival, I was thrilled to learn that the guest preacher and pianist was this same blind pianist, Peter. I walked up to him as he was rehearsing on the piano and said, "Guess who I am." He said, "David"; he had recognized my voice and remembered my name. How wonderful Christian fellowship is! We belong to each other, and we belong to the Lord Jesus.

I recall a Christian hymn entitled "He Knows My Name." My thoughts turn to John 10, when Jesus, the Good Shepherd, was talking to the Pharisees, who were antagonistic toward Him. Jesus explained to them, "I am the good shepherd, and know my sheep, and am known of mine" (v. 14).

Verses 3–4 read,

> The sheep hear his voice: and he calleth his own
> sheep by name, and leadeth them out. And when

he putteth forth his own sheep, he goeth before them, and the sheep follow him: for they know his voice.

Thank you, Lord. Once I was blind, but now I can see. The Light of the World is Jesus.

Remember

43

*Readings: Luke 23:32–43, 16:19–31,
22:54–62, and Jeremiah 31:34*

This is a reminder of God's faithfulness.

> On the battlefield, where they had suffered defeat,
> Israel pleaded with God for help, and He granted
> them a miraculous victory. Their priest and leader,
> Samuel, set up a monument to remind them of
> God's strong hand in their victory, and Samuel
> named the pillar Ebenezer, saying, "Thus far the
> LORD has helped us." (1 Samuel 7:12 NIV)

Each time the Israelites saw the Ebenezer stone, they
remembered God's help in the past, His help relied on for the
present, and His help assured for tomorrow. It reminded them
where to turn for their strength and power and to remember that
God was to be thanked for their deliverance.

One of the human frailties is forgetfulness, which was one of
the results of humanity's fall; it is one of God's complaints: "You

have forgotten Me." We read in Isaiah 49:15 that the Israelites said the Lord had forgotten and forsaken them, but the Lord replied,

> Can a woman forget her sucking child, that she should not have compassion on the son of her womb? yea, they may forget, yet will I not forget thee. Behold, I have graven thee upon the palms of my hands.

God does not forget us. Due to Jesus's sacrifice, He casts our sins behind Him and washes them as far as the east is from the west. He does not forget our sins; He positively "remembers them no more" (Hebrews 10:17).

God has led us "through the wilderness journey," through good times and bad. We should remember the blessings of life, parents, home, health, education, and family and especially those times in our lives when God turned what appeared to be disaster into an unexpected opportunity or when He took us through suffering and hardship so we would learn to trust Him more.

Our personal Ebenezer banishes fear, doubt, and disbelief today because we realize how many times in the past God has forgiven, protected, and guided us. Moses encouraged the children of Israel to remember His goodness.

> And thou shalt remember all the way which the Lord thy God led thee these forty years in the wilderness, to humble thee, and to prove thee, to know what was in thine heart, whether thou wouldest keep his commandments, or no. And he humbled thee, and suffered thee to hunger, and fed thee with manna, which thou knewest not, neither did thy fathers know; that he might make thee know that man doth not live by bread only, but by every word that proceedeth out of the

mouth of the Lord doth man live. (Deuteronomy 8:2–3)

As the Israelites did, we should remember how God has led us and praise Him for His mercy and grace.

When God made man and woman, He gave them five senses—touch, smell, sight, hearing, and taste. No wonder the psalmist could say in Psalm 139:14, "I will praise thee; for I am fearfully and wonderfully made; marvellous are thy works."

We can add to those five senses. He made us with minds, consciences, and memory. These capacities are important to our lives, and the older we get, the more we realize the importance of our memory. The Lord expects us to use our memories and has encouraged us to do so even in our youth. In Ecclesiastes 12:1, He said, "Remember now thy Creator in the days of thy youth, while the evil days come not."

Our conscience is like an alarm system so that we recognize our failures in the sight of God. And that should lead us to repentance. Yes, even believers need to repent.

A Remembrance of Repentance

In Luke 22:61, after Judas had betrayed Jesus, they led Jesus into the high priest's hall, and Peter stood far off and denied the Lord three times as he was warming himself by a fire. We see how his memory and conscience were acting together as he remembered what Jesus had told him.

> And the Lord turned and looked upon Peter. And Peter remembered the word of the Lord, how He had said unto him, Before the cock crow, thou shalt deny Me thrice. And Peter went out and wept bitterly.

That was a remembrance of repentance. Peter knew he had failed Jesus, whose penetrating look caused Peter to weep bitter tears of repentance. I think the penetrating look was also a loving and forgiving look, not an accusing look.

This reminds me of another look of the Lord Jesus. Riding on a colt a week before His crucifixion, "He beheld [looked upon] the city of Jerusalem and wept over it" because it had missed the opportunity to accept Him as its Messiah (Luke 19:41).

A Remembrance of Remorse

We read the parable of the rich man and Lazarus in Luke 16. It is not primarily a parable about our eternal state but rather a warning to the Pharisees about living covetous lives and ignoring God's claims. It was a warning to the religious leaders against complacency and self-sufficiency, against the "I'm all right, Jack" attitude leaving God out of their lives.

Appealing to Abraham, the rich man seeks mercy, but it is too late, and Abraham tells him, "Son, remember that thou in thy lifetime receivedst thy good things, and likewise Lazarus evil things: but now he is comforted, and thou art tormented" (Luke 16:25).

A Remembrance of Response

Two thieves were crucified alongside Jesus. One had nothing good to say about Jesus whereas the other in his dying moments trusted in Christ for his eternal salvation. His cry to Jesus on the cross was, "Lord, remember me when Thou comest into Thy kingdom" (Luke 23:42).

These are some of the things the penitent thief realized.

- He was a sinner: "We receive the due reward of our deeds."
- The perfection of Christ: "This man hath done nothing amiss."
- Jesus is a King with a kingdom not of this world.
- Jesus is Lord: "Lord, remember me."

How wonderful that the words of the thief were the same words of Jesus to His followers and to us to remember Him.

> And he took bread, and gave thanks, and brake it, and gave unto them, saying, this is my body which is given for you: this do in remembrance of me. Likewise, also the cup after supper, saying, this cup is the new testament in my blood, which is shed for you. (Luke 22:19–20)

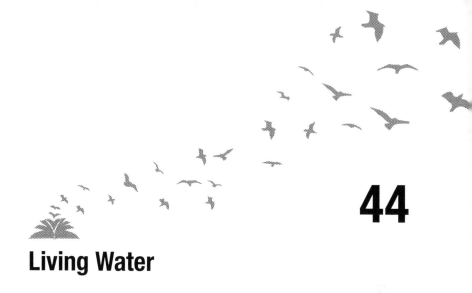

44

Living Water

Readings: John 4:1–19, 25–30, 39–42

The Importance of Water

The UN's World Water Day, which focuses on freshwater, has been held on March 22nd every year since 1993. The day celebrates water and raises awareness of the 2.2 billion people living without safe water. It is about taking action to tackle the global water crisis.

Consider water as liquid gold; it is so precious. Space explorations to Mars are being undertaken to discover whether there is water on that planet because scientists know that without water, life cannot exist. Water covers about 70 percent of the earth's surface, but 95 percent is saltwater not suitable for drinking. How ironic it is that someone could be surrounded by water and yet die of thirst because it is not fit to drink. In Greek mythology, one of Zeus's sons was condemned to stand chin-deep in water, and whenever he lowered his head to drink, it fled from him. His name was Tantalus, from which *tantalize* is derived.

We use the word *thirst* to describe a longing for something and not necessarily water; we can thirst after knowledge, success, justice, glory, and so on. In Matthew 5:6, Jesus said, "Blessed are they which do hunger and thirst after righteousness: for they shall be filled." Thirst can be regarded in a sense wider than just a lack of water.

In John 4, we read of the meeting of Jesus with the Samaritan woman, and the main thoughts are of the Savior of the world, the sinful woman, and the satisfying water.

The Savior of the World

Here, we can think of Jesus as the seeking Savior because He went out of His way to meet with this woman though she was unaware of that. Normally, a Jew would not travel through Samaria because the Jews "have no dealings with the Samaritans," but Paul reminded us in 1 Timothy 1:15 "that Christ Jesus came into the world to save sinners."

The Sinful Woman

Jesus met this woman when she came to draw water from the well at midday, a time when she could avoid seeing other women. She told Jesus that she had had five husbands and was living with a man who was not her husband. It sounds like she was ashamed to draw water when all the other women from the village came to draw water.

The Satisfying Water

Being human and thus subject to thirst and weariness, Jesus asked her for some water. The woman asked him why He, a Jew, would ask a Samaritan woman for a drink seeing that Jews had no dealings with Samaritans. Jesus said,

> If you knew the gift of God, and who it is who says
> to you, Give Me a drink, you would have asked
> Him, and He would have given you living water.
> (John 4:10–11 NASU)

What is the Living Water? Eternal life! Jesus explained in
John 4:13–14 (NASU),

> Everyone who drinks of this water will thirst
> again; but whoever drinks of the water that I will
> give him shall never thirst; but the water that I
> will give him will become in him a well of water
> springing up to eternal life.

She began wondering if Jesus was greater than Jacob, who
had established this well, or if Jesus was a prophet. She knew that
the Messiah was coming, and Jesus revealed to her that He was
indeed that Messiah.

The result of the conversation was that the woman realized
her greatest need was not for H_2O but for this Living Water. She
said, "Sir, give me this water, that I thirst not, neither come hither
to draw" (John 4:15).

The wells never dry up for the believer. Although they are
available to believers, they can be realized only if they draw on
them just as they would draw money from a bank. Our parched
and dry souls will be refreshed with the wells of salvation. Isaiah
trusted God.

> Behold, God is my salvation: I will trust, and not
> be afraid: for the Lord JEHOVAH is my strength
> and my song; he also is become my salvation.
> Therefore, with joy shall ye draw water out of the
> wells of salvation. (Isaiah 12:2)

In times of doubt, draw water from the well of assurance. Remember the promises of God and that they are all fulfilled in Jesus Christ, who is the "Yea" and "Amen" to all the promises of God. Get to know His promises.

In times of stress, draw water from the well of peace and joy. Jesus said, "Come to Me, all you who labour and are heavy laden, and I will give you rest" (Matthew 11:28–30 NKJV).

In times of despair, draw water from the well of eternal life and hope. Think about the empty tomb on the morning of the resurrection. Because of Jesus, we have a hope that goes beyond the grave.

In times of need, draw water from the well of provision and abundance. God has met our greatest need. In His Son, we do not have just life but abundant life! Learn to be content with what you have, and trust Jesus to provide your needs just as He promised.

In times of rejection, draw water from the well of knowing that you are accepted by God in the Beloved One even though you may be rejected by the world.

When I think of water being like liquid gold, I think of my three years in university studying economics and learning that the value of anything depends on the supply of and demand for it. If you were stranded in the middle of a desert and somebody offered to sell you some water, you would probably pay a large amount for it. And if someone else who needed water was there, the price would probably go up.

In Revelation 22:17, God invited the thirsty soul to drink the Water of Life.

> The Spirit and the bride say, Come, and let him
> that heareth say, Come. And let him that is athirst
> come. And whosoever will, let him take the water
> of life freely.

45

The Ascension

Reading: Luke 24:50–53

> And He led them out as far as to Bethany, and
> He lifted up His hands, and blessed them. And
> it came to pass, while He blessed them, He was
> parted from them, and carried up into heaven.
> And they worshipped Him and returned to
> Jerusalem with great joy: And were continually
> in the temple, praising and blessing God.

On Good Friday, there was the crucifixion, on Easter Sunday, the
resurrection, and forty days later, the ascension. Christ's ascension
has not received the attention it deserves though it was a crucial
part of His work. It made an enormous difference to the church all
through the church age, and it still does today because resources
are now available to the children of God for living fruitful lives
they would otherwise not have.

When we speak of the finished work of Christ, we think of
the cross and His resurrection, but His ascension and exaltation
were fundamental parts of God's purposes. The ascension brings

to completion His ministry on earth and the commencement of His work in heaven.

When Jesus told His disciples He would be leaving them soon, they were disturbed and puzzled, but His ascension had a profound effect on them; they were transformed, and it was with great joy that they returned to Jerusalem. They maintained a regular presence in the temple worshipping God; they were happy and filled with joy.

Jesus had encouraged them by teaching them about the ministry of the Holy Spirit.

> I will pray the Father, and He will give you another Helper, that He may abide with you forever—the Spirit of truth, I will not leave you orphans; I will come to you. (John 14:16–18 NKJV)

Perhaps that was why they were transformed. So, what is the significance of the ascension?

Jesus would be received into heaven to be with His Father.

While He was on the cross, His Father had forsaken Him because of our sin. He was God's beloved Son who had always dwelt in the bosom of the Father. Now, there would be a fanfare to welcome Jesus as the King of Glory. The psalmist prophesied the entry of Christ into heaven: "Lift up your heads, O ye gates; even lift them up, ye everlasting doors; and the King of glory shall come in" (Psalm 24:9).

He would receive the approval of His Father.

Jesus had fully accomplished His mission on earth. God highly exalted Him and set Him at His right hand. In keeping with His prayer in John 17:5, He would receive the glory that had been His before the foundation of the world. And there was the added glory of being the Savior and Mediator who had triumphed over sin and death.

Jesus's return to heaven established Jesus as the reigning King.

The ascension established His enthronement as the King who now rules with all authority. As Peter wrote, "[Jesus] who has gone into heaven and is on the right hand of God—angels and authorities and powers being made subject unto him" (1 Peter 3:22). He is King of Kings and Lord of Lords.

It marked the coming of the Holy Spirit.

Jesus promised that when He returned to heaven, the Father would not leave them comfortless and abandoned like orphans; He would send another Comforter, the Holy Spirit.

> That He may abide with you for ever; even the Spirit of truth whom the world cannot receive, because it seeth him not, neither knoweth him. But ye know Him; for He dwelleth with you and shall be in you. (John 14:16–17)

Jesus kept His promise, and on the Day of Pentecost, the Holy Spirit came down.

Our home in heaven is guaranteed.

One other benefit that should encourage believers is the knowledge that Jesus's homecoming was a pledge that guaranteed our homecoming to be with Jesus forever, for He said,

> In my Father's house are many mansions: if it were not so, I would have told you. I go to prepare a place for you. And if I go and prepare a place for you, I will come again, and receive you unto myself; that where I am, there ye may be also. (John 14:1–3)

Here are some precious truths that help us live fruitful lives that concern the work of the Holy Spirit in us. As believers, we have these resources of the Holy Spirit.

His Presence

The bodily presence of Christ has gone to heaven, but now, the Holy Spirit has come. His presence is not only with us but also indwells us; Jesus said, "He shall be in you" (John 14:17).

During His earthly ministry, Jesus's work was geographically limited, but now, He is omnipresent and able to hear and respond to His people's prayers no matter where they are.

His Power

We have access to His power. Just before He ascended, Jesus told His disciples, "But ye shall receive power, and ye shall be witnesses unto me both in Jerusalem, and in all Judaea, and in Samaria, and unto the uttermost part of the earth" (Acts 1:8). This power is available to us today.

His Guidance

He guides us along life's journey: "When the Spirit of truth is come, He will guide you into all truth" (John 16:13).

His Teaching

> But the Comforter shall teach you all things and bring all things to your remembrance whatsoever I have said unto you. (John 14:26)

His Intercession

He appears in heaven as our great High Priest and as our intercessor.

> For Christ is not entered into the holy places made with hands, which are the figures of the true; but into heaven itself, now to appear in the presence of God for us. (Hebrews 9:24)

We also read in Hebrews 4:14–16,

> Seeing then that we have a great high priest, let us therefore come boldly unto the throne of grace, that we may obtain mercy, and find grace to help in time of need.

We can now draw near for mercy, for grace and help when we are in need. He alone is the unique mediator between God and man (1 Timothy 2:5).

His Gifts to the Church

The church was instituted after His ascension to represent Him on earth. The Bible tells us that the church is His body and He is its Head.

In Ephesians 1:22–23 (NLT), writing about Jesus's resurrection and ascension, Paul said,

> God has put all things under the authority of Christ and has made him head over all things for the benefit of the church. And the church is his body; it is made full and complete by Christ, who fills all things everywhere with himself.

In Ephesians 4:10–12, Paul connected the gifts we've received with the ascension.

> He that descended is the same also that ascended up far above all heavens, that he might fill all things. And he gave some, apostles; and some, prophets; and some, evangelists; and some, pastors, and teachers; for the perfecting of the saints, for the work of the ministry, for the edifying of the body of Christ.

The ascended Lord Jesus will return as King and Judge.

In Acts 1:11 (ESV), two angels told the disciples, "This Jesus, who was taken up from you into heaven, will come in the same way as you saw him go into heaven."

Jesus's reign will one day be fully realized on earth (see Revelation 11:15, 19:10–16, 22:3). This is what we ask for when we pray, "Your kingdom come, your will be done, on earth as it is in heaven."

At His return, the Lord Jesus will execute divine judgment.

Now that we know the story, we can delve deeper into its importance and relevance for our lives and our faith.

Hope in a Glorious Future

The ascended Lord will return as judge and king. Then there will be a new heaven and earth. He will abolish injustice, end suffering, destroy death, and set up His kingdom of truth, righteousness, and love.

There were great voices in heaven, saying, The kingdoms of this world are become the kingdoms of our Lord, and of his Christ; and he shall reign for ever and ever. (Revelation 11:15–17)

Best of all, we will be with our King forever.

46

The Race Set before Us

Have you heard of Sir Mohamed Muktar Jama Faarax, CBE? He is better known as Mo Farah, a great British athlete. He officially retired when he was thirty-four. He was thinking of coming out of retirement to defend his record in the Olympic games to be held in Tokyo in 2021 but did not. Another athlete who retired when he was comparatively young (thirty-one) was Usain Bolt. In contrast, followers of the Lord Jesus do not retire from the race until they reach heaven. The race set before them is not a sprint but a marathon.

Caleb was eighty-five when the children of Israel entered the Promised Land. Moses and Abraham were also quite old when their races were completed.

Of Moses, we read in Hebrews 11:27 that "by faith he forsook Egypt, not fearing the wrath of the king; for he endured as seeing Him who is invisible" and in Deuteronomy 34:7, "Moses was an hundred and twenty years old when he died, his eye was not dim, nor his natural force abated."

Abraham was willing to go wherever God led him through countries in which he was a stranger because "he looked for a city which hath foundations whose builder and maker is God"

(Hebrews 11:10). Surely this task required endurance as well as faith. In Hebrews 6:15, we read this about Abraham: "After he had patiently endured, he obtained the promise." He was 175 when he died.

Both these patriarchs had their eyes fixed on their goal. Abraham "looked for a city whose builder and maker was God" and "Moses endured as seeing Him who is invisible." He had His eyes on God.

The race the writer to the Hebrews was referring to is found in chapter 12; it is a marathon that requires patient endurance. The characters in the previous chapter, Hebrews 11, were witnesses to us of the patient endurance as well as faith required in life's marathon. They are set out before us as examples to encourage us to persevere, to endure in our lives of service and commitment to God even though the going may be tough.

Jesus Himself was referred to as a runner. In Hebrews 6:20, we read that He went in advance of His followers, who were to be where He was when He came to receive them to Himself. "The forerunner is for us entered [within the veil], even Jesus, made an high priest for ever after the order of Melchizedec." He has run the race before us and is waiting to receive us.

Athletes prepare for the race by eating the right food. How important it is for us believers to eat the right food. What we see on TV and read in books and newspapers is often what we digest just like food. We should ask ourselves if it is good food that helps us grow in our faith.

Believers should prepare for the race by laying aside every incumbrance and every sin to which they are prone. In Hebrews 12, we read, "Let us run with patient endurance the race that is set before us."

There may be times when we stumble along the road, but Isaiah shows us what to do in such a case.

He giveth power to the faint; and to them that
have no might He increaseth strength. Even the
youths shall faint and be weary, and the young
men shall utterly fall: But they that wait upon the
Lord shall renew their strength; they shall mount
up with wings as eagles; they shall run, and not be
weary; and they shall walk, and not faint. (Isaiah
40:29–31)

Runners do not look at spectators or other competitors,
and they may see the finish line, but their minds are fixed
on the prize, the gold medal. Christians' eyes should be on
the prize, Christ. Here, the runner is "looking unto Jesus, the
author and finisher of faith" (Hebrews 12:3). Without Jesus,
faith is redundant and of no consequence for He is its author
and completer. The prize for Christians is to know Christ and
behold Him in all His glory.

In Philippians 3:10–11 (NLT), we read of Paul's goal.

I want to know Christ and experience the mighty
power that raised him from the dead … I want to
suffer with him, sharing in his death, so that one
way or another I will experience the resurrection
from the dead!

In Psalm 27:4, David declared his ambition.

One thing have I desired of the Lord, that will
I seek after; that I may dwell in the house of the
Lord all the days of my life, to behold the beauty
of the Lord.

In Hebrews 12:2–3, we see Jesus as our great example of
endurance.

> Who for the joy that was set before Him, endured
> the cross, despising the shame, and is set down at
> the right hand of the throne of God. For consider
> Him who endured such contradiction of sinners
> against Himself, lest ye be wearied and faint in
> your minds.

Jesus endured the cross, the great example of patient endurance. What was His goal? Why did He endure the cross? The answer is, "For the joy that was set before Him."

When the Olympic games were held in Barcelona some years ago, the world saw one of the greatest moments in Olympic history. Derek Redmond was a young athlete from Britain who had worked hard to get to the Olympics, and his dream was within his reach. He was in the semifinals of the 400 meters, and he was running the race of his life. He saw the finish line as he rounded the final bend. Suddenly, he felt a sharp pain in his leg and fell; he had torn a muscle.

As the medical attendants ran toward him, he struggled to his feet and started to hop toward the finish line. Jim's father pushed aside a steward and ran to Derek's side. "You don't have to do this," he told his son. "Yes, I do," said Derek. "Well, then," said his father, "we'll finish this race together." And they did. They stayed in Derek's lane all the way to the end. At first, the crowd watched in silence, but then they rose to their feet and cheered.

What was the joy set before Jesus as He faced the agony of the cross? Was it worthwhile? Yes, it was. It brought satisfaction to the heart of God. We read in Isaiah 53:10–11, "The pleasure of Jehovah shall prosper in His hand; He shall see of the travail of His soul and shall be satisfied."

It also brought the reunion with His Father in glory. John 17:5 reads, "O Father, glorify Thou me with thine own self, with the glory which I had with Thee before the world was."

Jesus asked the two disciples in Emmaus, "Ought not Christ to have suffered these things and to enter into His glory?" (Luke 24:26).

Praise the Lord! What a prospect!

God's Requirement

47

Reading: Deuteronomy 10:12–13

> What doth the Lord require of thee, but to fear
> the Lord thy God, to walk in all His ways, and
> to love Him, and to serve the Lord thy God with
> all thy heart and with all thy soul, to keep the
> commandments of the Lord and His statutes.

These were the words Moses spoke to the children of Israel to
encourage them. He had spent forty days and forty nights pleading
with God to spare His people because they had provoked Him
by making a golden calf while Moses was receiving the Ten
Commandments. How ungrateful was that? It was Jehovah who
had saved them from slavery in Egypt.

Moses was their mediator pleading for the people. We also
have a mediator, an intercessor who pleads on our behalf—the
Lord Jesus.

> How much more shall the blood of Christ, who
> through the eternal Spirit offered Himself without

spot to God, cleanse your conscience from dead works to serve the living God? And for this reason, He is the Mediator of the new covenant. (Hebrews 9:14–15 NKJV)

Moses had been given an insight into what God required of His people, and I believe this is exactly what God requires of us today.

Five things are mentioned in Deuteronomy 10.

Reverence: "to fear the Lord thy God"

We are to fear God but not in the sense of being afraid of Him. We are His children, and He is our Father. The word *fear* in this sense means "to reverence," "to stand in awe of," and to remember who He is—the Creator of all things and the one to whom we will have to give an account one day.

Consistency: "to walk in all His ways"

Many verses in the Bible refer to our walk as believers. I think we could emphasize the little word *all* here—to walk in *all* His ways following His footsteps.

The following list describes how believers should walk.

- We should walk in newness of life. (Romans 6:4)
- Let us walk honestly. (Romans 13:13)
- Let us also walk in the Spirit. (Galatians 5:25)
- Walk worthy of the vocation wherewith ye are called. (Ephesians 4:1)
- And walk in love, as Christ also hath loved us. (Ephesians 5:2)
- Walk as children of light. (Ephesians 5:8)

- Walk circumspectly, not as fools, but as the wise. (Ephesians 5:15)
- Walk in wisdom, redeeming the time. (Colossians 4:5)
- Walk even as He walked. (1 John 2:6)
- Walk in truth. (John 3:4)

What a comfort to know that wherever the Lord leads us, He will be with us even in the path of adversity or in the valley of the shadow of death.

> And though the Lord give you the bread of adversity and the water of affliction, yet your Teacher will not hide himself anymore, but your eyes shall see your Teacher. And your ears shall hear a word behind you, saying, this is the way, walk in it, when you turn to the right or when you turn to the left. (Isaiah 30:20–22 ESV)

> Yea, though I walk through the valley of the shadow of death, I will fear no evil: for thou art with me; thy rod and thy staff they comfort me. (Psalm 23:4)

Devotion: "to love Him"

To love somebody but not to be loved in return hurts, and God hurts because of unrequited love. Jesus wept over Jerusalem because the people had spurned His love.

There is a lovely gospel song that starts like this: "Oh, how He loves you and me. He gave His life; what more could He give?" Deuteronomy 10 says that God requires us to love Him. Jesus asked Peter not for money, respect, or admiration but for his love. "Peter, do you love me?" (John 21:15–17 NKJV).

He deserves our love. Paul said, "We love Him because He first loved us" (1 John 4:19).

> For the Father himself loves you dearly because you love me and believe that I came from God. (John 16:27 NLT)

Service: "to serve the Lord with all thy heart"

When Israel sinned against God, Samuel interceded for its people so they would be spared God's judgment. He told them,

> Fear not: ye have done all this wickedness: yet turn not aside from following the Lord but serve the Lord with all your heart; and turn ye not aside. (1 Samuel 12:20)

In John 12:26, Jesus said,

> If any man serve Me, let him follow Me; and where I am, there shall also my servant be; if any man serve Me, him will my Father honour.

> Let us have grace, whereby we may serve God acceptably with reverence and godly fear. (Hebrews 12:28)

Our ambition should be to serve the Lord profitably so we may receive His commendation, "Well done, good and faithful servant; enter into the joy of thy Lord."

Obedience: "to keep the commandments of the Lord"

John 14:21 reads, "He that hath my commandments, and keepeth them, He it is that loveth me." In 1 John 5:3, we read, "This is the love of God that we keep His commandments: His commandments are not grievous."

> Ye have obeyed from the heart that form of doctrine which was delivered you. (Romans 6:17)

> O that my ways may be steadfast in keeping thy statutes! Then I shall not be put to shame, having my eyes fixed on all thy commandments. I will praise thee with an upright heart when I learn thy righteous ordinances. I will observe thy statutes. (Psalm 119:5–8 RSV)

The Lord Jesus asked Peter three times "Peter, do you love me?"

Here is a prayer for each day.

Lord, I love you. Please help me to trust and obey.
Lord, I love you. Please help me to trust and obey.
Lord, I love you. Please help me to trust and obey.

48

Paul's Motivation

I love the letter Paul wrote to the Philippians because it contains an abundance of themes; it exudes joy and rejoicing, it deals with the furtherance of the gospel, and it expresses the sufficiency of Christ in all situations.

Paul, a very educated man, was a Jew brought up in Damascus, a Gentile city. He was a Roman citizen and had been influenced by Greek culture. We see evidence of all these influences in his writings in the New Testament. He was taught the strict legalism of the Pharisees under Gamaliel, which produced in Saul a zeal to persecute followers of "the [Christian] way."

But there came that day when Paul (Saul as he was known then) was on his way to Damascus with letters from the high priest giving him power to arrest and bring to Jerusalem followers of Christ. It was then that God's grace arrested him in his fanatical pursuit.

In Acts 9:4–6 (RSV), we read that he heard a voice, which only he heard, saying, "Saul, Saul, why do you persecute Me?" Saul replied, "Who art Thou, Lord?" And the Lord said, "I am Jesus of Nazareth whom you are persecuting." That was the moment of his conversion; his life was never the same after that.

He would have new ambitions and a new Master; he would have a completely new life. And his main motivation was driven by love for the Lord Jesus. A trembling Saul asked, "Lord, what wilt Thou have me to do?"

In his writings in the New Testament, he acknowledged that he had been saved by the grace and mercy of God (1 Timothy 1:14–16). After his conversion, he, the most learned and at the same time the humblest of the apostles (Ephesians 3:8; 1 Corinthians 15:9), was the one whose writings were most used in the New Testament scriptures.

In his letter to the Philippians, we get an insight into Paul's persona, drive, and ambition. I will take a verse or two from each chapter of Paul's letter to illustrate what made him tick and how his life should inspire us to live as believers.

We are reminded of

- His Position in Christ (1)
- His Pattern like Christ (2)
- His Priority for Christ (3)
- His Power through Christ (4)
- His Provision by Christ (4)

His Position in Christ (1:1)

Paul commenced his letter with "Paul and Timotheus, the servants of Jesus Christ, to all the saints in Christ Jesus which are at Philippi." Paul was writing to believers in Philippi, a strong Roman colony, but he referred to them and by implication himself as being in Christ. We often hear the expression, "You can't be in two places at once." Well, how wonderful! We can because we are also in Christ. Why is that so wonderful? Paul's letter to the Ephesians often refers to believers as being "in Christ."

For example, in Ephesians 2:6, he wrote, "[God] hath raised

us up together, and made us sit together in heavenly places in Christ Jesus." It is wonderful because that is the sphere of our blessings, which are found "in heavenly places in Christ."

The unsaved are interested primarily in earthly things because that is where they live; Jesus called them "the children of this world" (Luke 16:8). In contrast, the life of the Christian is centered in heaven. Our citizenship is in heaven (Philippians 3:20), our names are written in heaven (Luke 10:20), our Father is in heaven, and our attention and affection ought to be centered on the things of heaven.

Is that true of me? It was true of Paul. In his letter to the Colossians, Paul wrote,

> If ye then be risen with Christ, seek those things which are above, where Christ sitteth on the right hand of God. Set your affection on things above, not on things on the earth. (Colossians 3:1–2)

Paul knew the reality of this, and that is why he gave this advice to the believers in Colosse. We should always remember this and praise God.

His Pattern Like Christ (2:5–9)

> Let this mind be in you, which was also in Christ Jesus: Who, being in the form of God, thought it not robbery to be equal with God; but made himself of no reputation, and took upon him the form of a servant, and was made in the likeness of men: And being found in fashion as a man, he humbled himself, and became obedient unto death, even the death of the cross. Wherefore God

also hath highly exalted him and given him a name which is above every name.

Jesus showed extreme humility, and this was the pattern Paul followed to be like Christ. Paul had plenty to boast about and yet he was humble.

> Unto me, who am less than the least of all saints, is this grace given, that I should preach among the Gentiles the unsearchable riches of Christ. (Ephesians 3:8)

> This is a faithful saying, and worthy of all acceptation, that Christ Jesus came into the world to save sinners; of whom I am chief. (1 Timothy 1:15)

Paul was humble, and he said, "Let this mind be in you" like Christ.

His Priority for Christ (3)

In chapter 3, we see Paul's priority in life, that it should be above all things lived for Christ.

> Though I might also have confidence in the flesh. If any other man thinketh that he hath whereof he might trust in the flesh, I more; circumcised the eighth day of the stock of Israel, of the tribe of Benjamin, an Hebrew of the Hebrews; as touching the law, a Pharisee; concerning zeal, persecuting the church; touching the righteousness, which is in the law, blameless. But what things were gain to me, those I counted loss for Christ. (vv. 4–7)

All that Paul had once boasted about meant nothing to him; his priority was "all for Christ."

His Power through Christ (4)

In chapter 4:13, Paul wrote, "I can do all things through Christ which strengtheneth me."

When Paul asked the Lord three times to take away the thorn in his flesh, some unspecified physical problem, he said,

> The Lord said unto me, My grace is sufficient for thee: for my strength is made perfect in weakness. Most gladly therefore will I rather glory in my infirmities, that the power of Christ may rest upon me. Therefore, I take pleasure in infirmities, in reproaches, in necessities, in persecutions, in distresses for Christ's sake: for when I am weak, then am I strong. (2 Corinthians 12:9–10)

His Provision by Christ (4)

In 4:19, we see where Paul's supplies came from; he wrote, "But my God shall supply all your need according to His riches in glory by Christ Jesus."

Praise God that He is never impoverished by giving because all our needs are supplied by Christ, and He has endless resources. So let us remember the five things that should motivate us.

What Think Ye of Christ?

In the Bible, Jesus was constantly asking questions. Of course, He knew the answers, but by asking questions, He was getting His hearers to think for themselves and consider the issues of life. His teaching was riddled with questions.

One of the complaints God had against His people was "My people doth not consider ..." (Isaiah 1:3). In verse 18, God said, "Come now, and let us reason together."

Indeed, the Lord often marveled that the people of His day did not understand so many things; He had to ask them, "Why don't you understand?" It was a continual marvel to our Lord that men should be so ignorant. "How is it that ye do not understand?" (Matthew 16:11). "How think ye?" (Matthew 18:12). "What shall it profit a man?" (Mark 8:36).

The crucial question everyone must answer is the one Jesus asked the Pharisees, "What do you think of the Christ?" (Matthew 22:42 RSV). The American author Bruce Barton correctly called Jesus "the man nobody knows."

It was John Newton, the converted slave trader, who penned these words: "What think you of Christ? is the test; to try both your state and your scheme. You cannot be right in the rest, unless you think rightly of Him." Jesus asked the Pharisees this question, and down through the ages, people have been asking this same question. There has been a lot of confusion about who Jesus is.

His disciples had already told Jesus what people in general said of Him—that He was John the Baptist, or Elijah, even Jeremiah, or some other prophet (Matthew 16:14). Jesus confronted His disciples with the same question about His identity and asked them to make up their minds about Him. It was not enough that they should just accept the current opinion of the masses. Jesus asked them, "but who do you say that I am?"

Speaking for the group, Peter said Jesus was "the Christ, the Son of the living God" (Matthew 16:16). Jesus confirmed that Peter was right and that it had been revealed to Peter, an uneducated fisherman, by God.

For two thousand years, men have been talking and thinking about Jesus; some have their minds made up about who He is, and doubtless others have not. And though all these years have passed, this question comes up again addressed to each of us, today: "What do you think of Christ?"

There is a TV program in the UK called *Who Do You Think You Are?* The way to find out is by asking those people who know you best, and so it is with Jesus. We can listen to the comments of those who knew Jesus, His enemies and His friends, when we ask them, "What think ye of Christ?"

First among the witnesses are the Pharisees, who we know hated the Lord. Let us put a few questions to them. "Tell us, Pharisees, what you have against the Son of God. What do you think of Christ?"

This is their reply. "This man receives sinners and eats with them."

What an argument to bring against Him. Why, that is the very thing that makes us love Him. It is one of the greatest compliments ever paid Him.

In the church to which I belonged in Staffordshire was an

elderly couple, and the husband, every time Luke 15:2 was quoted, would say that his wife's name was mentioned in the Bible. "And the Pharisees and scribes murmured, saying, This man receiveth sinners, and eateth with them." He would say, "This man receiveth sinners and Edith with them." How true! This is the crux of the gospel. He receives sinners. If He had not, what would have become of us?

What does Caiaphas have to say? "Caiaphas, you were the chief priest, and you were the leader of the Sanhedrin when Christ was tried. You were there when they found Him guilty. It was you who condemned Him. Tell us, what did the witnesses say? On what grounds did you judge Him? What evidence was brought against Him?"

Caiaphas would respond by saying, "I said to him,"

> Art thou the Christ, the Son of the Blessed? And Jesus said, I am, and ye shall see the Son of man sitting on the right hand of power and coming in the clouds of heaven. Then the high priest rent his clothes, and saith, What need we any further witnesses? Ye have heard the blasphemy: what think ye? And they all condemned him to be guilty of death. (Mark 14:61–64)

The only case they had against Jesus was that He claimed to be the Son of God, and that indeed was the truth anyway.

How about Pilate? "Pilate, what do you have to say about Jesus?"

Pilate, a Gentile, would say, "I find no fault in this man" (Luke 23:4).

There is another important witness, a man who claimed to be a follower of Christ, the betrayer, Judas Iscariot. "Judas, what do you have to say concerning this one whom you betrayed? You were with Him when He performed many miracles, yet you betrayed Him for thirty pieces of silver. What do you have to say now?"

Judas realizes the enormity of what he had done and says, "I have betrayed innocent blood" (Matthew 27:34).

There are many more witnesses we could ask. There was the centurion responsible for carrying out the execution of Jesus. Having witnessed all the events on that dreadful day, he exclaimed, "Truly this was the Son of God" (Matthew 27:54).

God opened heaven to declare on at least three occasions, "This is My beloved Son" (Matthew 17:5).

As we read the scriptures, the overwhelming evidence confirms that Jesus is the Christ, the Son of the Living God.

50

The Good Shepherd

Reading: John 10:9–11, 14–15, 17–18, 24–26, 27–30

I am the door: by me if any man enters in, he shall be saved, and shall go in and out, and find pasture. I am come that they might have life, and that they might have it more abundantly. I am the good shepherd: the good shepherd giveth his life for the sheep.

I am the good shepherd, and know my sheep, and am known of mine. As the Father knoweth me, even so know I the Father: and I lay down my life for the sheep.

Therefore doth my Father love me, because I lay down my life, that I might take it again. No man taketh it from me, but I lay it down of myself. I have power to lay it down, and I have power to take it again. This commandment have I received of my Father.

> Then came the Jews round about him, and said
> unto him, how long dost thou make us to doubt? If
> thou be the Christ, tell us plainly. Jesus answered
> them, I told you, and ye believed not: the works
> that I do in my Father's name, they bear witness
> of me. But ye believe not, because ye are not of
> my sheep, as I said unto you.
>
> My sheep hear my voice, and I know them, and
> they follow me: And I give unto them eternal life;
> and they shall never perish, neither shall any man
> pluck them out of my hand. My Father, which
> gave them me, is greater than all; and no man is
> able to pluck them out of my Father's hand. I and
> my Father are one.

Jesus often spoke in parables taking illustrations from everyday life to explain things relating to the kingdom of heaven, earthly stories with a heavenly meaning. Very often, using figurative language, Jesus likened Himself to many things. For example, He said He was the Way, the Truth, and the Life. The Bread of Life. The Light of the World. The True Vine.

In John 10, Jesus likened Himself to a shepherd and to the door of the sheepfold. In biblical times, shepherds led their sheep not as today when shepherds follow their sheep. Also, when sheep were out on the mountainside, shepherds would have sheepfolds built of stones, pens where the sheep could find shelter from storms and wild beasts. Sheepfolds had no doors except that the shepherd would lay across the entrance and would in effect become the door. By doing so, he was putting himself at risk trying to protect his flock from marauding animals.

In verses 11 and 14, Jesus said, "I am the Good Shepherd; the Good Shepherd gives his life for the sheep." He also said, "I know my sheep, and my sheep know Me." And again, as the

Good Shepherd, He said, "I lay down my life for the sheep." As we think of Jesus as the Good Shepherd, we see Him as one who knows His sheep by name, and they know Him, recognize His voice, and follow Him.

Jesus told His disciples to rejoice because their names were written in heaven, in the Book of Life. Is your name recorded in heaven as one of God's children, as one of His sheep? Do you know the Shepherd as your Savior? David the psalmist was able to say, "The Lord is my Shepherd."

We see Jesus in our reading as the door of the sheepfold. He is the way into God's safekeeping and protection, into heaven. Just as the shepherd would lay down at the entrance to the sheepfold to protect his sheep and even if necessary, die for them, Jesus said, "I am the door, I lay down My life for the sheep." Jesus was referring to the fact that He was about to lay down His life on the cruel cross of Calvary to save sinners like us from the judgment of a thrice-holy God. Praise God Jesus went on to say, "I lay down my life that I may take it again." In other words, I will rise again from the dead.

In relation to every believer, these are wonderful truths in which we can rejoice.

Three words describe the death of Jesus. His was a *voluntary* death; He laid down His life. No man took His life from Him; He laid it down Himself.

It was a *vicarious* death in that it took the place of another. The apostle Paul wrote in his letter to the Christians in Galatia, "The Son of God who loved me and gave Himself for me" (Galatians 2:20). In Isaiah 53:6, we read, "All we like sheep have gone astray; we have turned everyone to his own way; and the Lord hath laid on him the iniquity of us all." He died for me, and He died for you.

His death was a *victorious* death. He said, "I have power to lay it down, and I have power to take it again. This commandment have I received of my Father." Praise God He rose from the dead on the third day as the victorious and living Savior able to give to undeserving sinners eternal life on the basis that He died to bear the penalty for their sins.

Paul recorded in 1 Corinthians 15:54–57,

> Death is swallowed up in victory. O death, where is thy sting? O grave, where is thy victory? The sting of death is sin; and the strength of sin is the law. But thanks be to God, which giveth us the victory through our Lord Jesus Christ.

In John 10:27–30, we read of eternal life and the security of the believer. We read that that no man can pluck the believer out of the hand of the Lord Jesus or out of His Father's hand.

In John 14:1–3, Jesus said,

> Let not your heart be troubled: ye believe in God, believe also in me. In my Father's house are many mansions: if it were not so, I would have told you. I go to prepare a place for you that where I am there shall you be also.

The Lord keeps His promises. "In God We Trust" is the official motto of the United States adopted by the US Congress in 1956. Would that it was the motto of all nations.

51

To Whom Am I Accountable?

Readings: Luke 20:19–26, Matthew 22:21

The scribes and pharisees wanted to trap Jesus into saying something worthy of arrest by the Roman occupying rulers of the land of Palestine. Perhaps they could tempt Jesus into saying something that would offend the Romans, perhaps something seditious speaking against the authority of Caesar or even something worthy of His execution.

So they came up with this question: "Is it lawful to pay taxes to Caesar or not?" (Matthew 22:17 NKJV). Perhaps they thought Jesus would say that it was not lawful to give taxes to Caesar. However, Jesus confounded them with His answer. He asked for a Roman coin and asked whose image and name were on it. They told Him, "Caesar's." "Render therefore to Caesar the things that are Caesar's, and to God the things that are God's" (Matthew 22:21 NKJV).

What Jesus said was relevant to us today. His answer clearly showed that we have a responsibility to the authorities who govern us locally or nationally. The Bible tells us that the "powers that be are ordained of God."

Peter wrote in 1 Peter 2:13–17 (NIV),

> Submit yourselves for the Lord's sake to every
> authority instituted among men: whether to the
> king, as the supreme authority, or to governors,
> who are sent by him to punish those who do
> wrong and to commend those who do right.

Paul wrote the same thing in Romans 13:1–8 (NIV).

> Everyone must submit himself to the governing
> authorities, for there is no authority except that
> which God has established. The authorities that
> exist have been established by God. Consequently,
> he who rebels against the authority is rebelling
> against what God has instituted, and those who do
> so will bring judgment on themselves. This is also
> why you pay taxes, for the authorities are God's
> servants, who give their full time to governing.
> Give everyone what you owe him: If you owe taxes,
> pay taxes; if revenue, then revenue; if respect,
> then respect; if honour, then honour. Let no debt
> remain outstanding, except the continuing debt to
> love one another, for he who loves his fellowman
> has fulfilled the law.

What surprised the scribes and pharisees about Jesus's answer
was not so much that He agreed taxes ought to be paid to Caesar
but rather that He had raised the question of responsibility to
a higher authority, God. Even Caesar was accountable to God
though he had his subjects bow to him as if he were a god.

So, to whom are we accountable in this life? We have a
responsibility to the authorities who govern us and a responsibility
to God, but there is a big difference between the two. Our

responsibility to God will affect our eternal destiny whereas our responsibility to the state affects only our condition during this earthly life.

However, the statements of both Paul and Peter are not the final word since Peter and other disciples, after they were forbidden by the authorities to preach the gospel, continued to do so, stating before the council of Jewish leaders that they ought to obey God rather than men (Acts 5:29), acknowledging the higher authority of God. This is why we believe freedom of conscience is important and that God's Word should be the final arbiter.

In regard to the accountability to God, Jesus said, "Render unto God the things which belong to God" (Matthew 22:21).

In Psalm 116:12, we read, "What shall I render unto the Lord for all His benefits toward me?" *Render* means "to give" or "give back." This suggests that we have taken from God what He expects and demands. We have rebelled against Him by sinning and refusing to acknowledge Him for who He is—the almighty Creator. We have dethroned Him and set ourselves on the throne. It is as if we said, "We will not have this man Jesus to reign over us but Caesar." This reminds me of God's complaint in Malachi 3:8: "Will a man rob God? Yet ye have robbed me. But ye say, wherein have we robbed thee?" Jesus answered that question: "Give back to God the things which belong to God." What things? For a start, recognition that He is the only true God. And when we appreciate who He is, we will give Him the respect and honor due Him.

We should give Him His rightful place as Lord and King in our lives. Sadly, some live as though they have said, "I don't want God in my life. I don't want this man Jesus to reign over me. I want Barabbas. I want Caesar. I want Mammon. I want sin." We have rebelled against God and Jesus Christ. How sad, and how disastrous. It is an imperative that we hold ourselves responsible to God for at least three reasons. First, He is our Creator. Second, He is our Redeemer. Third, He is our Judge before whom we will stand one day.

We are accountable to God because He is our Creator. There is a growing spread of the theory of evolution and the denial of God as the Creator. However, the Bible clearly teaches that God created all things. We read in Genesis 1:26 that God said, "Let us make man in our own image."

In his gospel, John stated that all things were created by Him and that without Him, nothing was made that was made. As our Creator, He expects us to honor and respect Him and give Him His due: "Give unto the Lord the glory due unto his name; worship the Lord in the beauty of holiness" (Psalm 29:2). The most important of His commandments as Jesus confirmed was that we should love Him with all our hearts, souls, minds, and strength.

In John's vision recorded in Revelation, he saw and heard those gathered around the heavenly throne worshipping the Lamb of God with these words.

> You are worthy, our Lord and God, to receive glory and honour and power, for you created all things, and by your will they were created and have their being. (Revelation 4:11 NIV)

We are accountable to Him because He is our Redeemer. He redeemed us; He paid a price to save us from slavery. This is the heart of the gospel message. He has a claim on us because He has paid a price for us.

In Isaiah 43:1, God was reminding His people that they belonged to Him because He had created them and redeemed them from slavery.

> But now thus saith the Lord that created thee, O Jacob, and he that formed thee, O Israel, Fear not: for I have redeemed thee, I have called thee by thy name; thou art mine.

We have already defined the word *render* as "to give back." It infers that the true owner is deprived of a possession. The word *redeemer* has a similar meaning; when God redeemed His people from slavery in Egypt, He was effectively buying them back.

In modern times, the word *redeem* is not commonly used, but most people would associate it with pawn shops. Those who need money can exchange an object of some value for a loan and then later buy back the object by paying the loan with interest.

I remember a story from when I was a boy about how a young lad made a boat out of wood and bits and pieces, and he was so proud of it. But he lost it, and one day, he found it displayed in a shop window. He had to pay the shopkeeper to regain ownership of it; he redeemed it. That is a picture of how God, who created humankind as His great masterpiece; lost His beautiful creation because of sin. But then He bought us back by paying the price for our redemption when Jesus died on the cross.

In heaven, they sing a new song.

> And they sung a new song, saying, Thou art worthy to take the book, and to open the seals thereof: for thou wast slain, and hast redeemed us to God by thy blood out of every kindred, and tongue, and people, and nation. And hast made us unto our God kings and priests: and we shall reign on the earth. (Revelation 5:9–10)

We are accountable to God judicially. One day, we will come before Him as our Judge. Hebrews 9:27 reads, "It is appointed unto men once to die but after this the judgement."

> God commands all people everywhere to repent. For he has set a day when he will judge the world

with justice by the man he has appointed. He has given proof of this to all men by raising him from the dead. (Acts 17:30–31 NIV)

I said in a previous chapter that justice is getting what we deserve, mercy is not getting what we deserve, and grace is getting what we do not deserve. In Psalm 103, we are reminded that God is a god of justice, mercy, and grace. Why should we bless the Lord? Psalm 103 (NKJV) gives us some very good answers to that question.

> Bless the Lord, O my soul, and forget not all his benefits: Who forgives all your iniquities; who heals all thy diseases; Who redeems your life from destruction; who crowns you with lovingkindness and tender mercies; Who satisfies your mouth with good things; so that your youth is renewed like the eagle's.
>
> The Lord executes righteousness and judgment for all that are oppressed. The Lord is merciful and gracious, slow to anger, and plenteous in mercy. The Lord executes righteousness and justice for all who are oppressed. The Lord is merciful and gracious, slow to anger, and abounding in mercy. He will not always strive with us, nor will He keep His anger forever. He has not dealt with us according to our sins, nor punished us according to our iniquities.
>
> For as far as the heavens are high above the earth, so great is His mercy toward those who fear Him; as far as the east is from the wests so far has He

removed our transgressions from us. As a father pities his children so the Lord pities those who fear Him, for He knows our frame; He remembers that we are dust.

52

Blind Bartimaeus

I want to tell you about Bartimaeus, a man who met Jesus Christ in real life. We read about him in Mark 10:46–52.

> And they came to Jericho: and as he went out of Jericho with his disciples and a great number of people, blind Bartimaeus, the son of Timaeus, sat by the highway side begging. And when he heard that it was Jesus of Nazareth, he began to cry out, and say, Jesus, thou Son of David, have mercy on me.

> And many charged him that he should hold his peace: but he cried the more a great deal, Thou Son of David, have mercy on me. And Jesus stood still and commanded him to be called. And they call the blind man, saying unto him, be of good comfort, rise; he calleth thee.

> And he, casting away his garment, rose, and came to Jesus. And Jesus answered and said unto him,

What wilt thou that I should do unto thee? The blind man said unto him, Lord, that I might receive my sight. And Jesus said unto him, Go thy way; thy faith hath made thee whole. And immediately he received his sight and followed Jesus in the way.

Bartimaeus had been born blind and had to beg for a living by the roadside. That is where he was the day Jesus was passing through Jericho with His disciples. There was a great crowd following Jesus, as He had been performing miracles healing the sick, probably including blind people.

Jesus had recently raised a girl to life after she had died. His power was so great that people were wondering who He was. A prophet? A great man of God? The Bible makes it clear that Jesus was and is indeed unique, the Son of God with the power to calm the raging sea, walk on water, cast out demons, and forgive sins.

Bartimaeus cried out, "Jesus, Thou Son of David, have mercy on me!" His friends thought that it was a lost cause, that Jesus would never hear Bartimaeus's feeble cry nor would be interested in him, so they told him to shut up. But Bartimaeus was not going to be put off. He shouted louder, and to the amazement of all, Jesus stood still and called Bartimaeus to come. He threw off his dirty cloak and very likely his stick so they would not encumber him, and jumping to his feet, he went to Jesus.

Jesus asked Bartimaeus what he wanted. He said, "I want to be able to see." Jesus said, "Go thy way. Thy faith hath made thee whole." And immediately he received his sight and followed Jesus in the way (Mark 10:52). Bartimaeus recognized that Jesus was the Son of David, another name for the Messiah, the Son of God, and he believed Jesus was able to heal him. And that is why Jesus said, "Thy faith hath made thee whole." The first person he saw with his new eyes was Jesus, and the Bible says that he followed Jesus, no doubt absolutely thrilled and rejoicing.

In many ways, Bartimaeus is a picture of you and me. We saw first his condition; he was a blind beggar. The Bible says that though we may have physical sight, our minds are blinded if we do not know Jesus as our Savior. We read in 2 Corinthians 4:4,

> The god of this world [Satan] hath blinded the minds of them which believe not, lest the light of the glorious gospel of Christ, who is the image of God, should shine unto them.

When Saul was converted to the Christian faith on the road to Damascus, he saw the risen Jesus, who commissioned him to preach the gospel to the nations, telling him to "turn them from darkness to light" (Acts 26:18).

Is your mind so blind that you cannot appreciate who Jesus is and why He died on a cross? The message of the gospel is so simple; He died to bear the punishment for our sin. He who had no sin died for us sinners so that if we believe in Him, if we trust Him, we should have eternal life.

So you see, unbelievers are blind. They are also beggars. Without Christ in their lives, they have nothing to bring to God, their Maker, and they certainly have nothing to merit eternal life. If we are trusting the Lord, we were once in that condition, but praise God, things are different now.

Sins cannot be paid for by good works, by church attendance—by any effort of ourselves. The Bible says the best we can offer God is filthy rags just like the beggar's rags.

Bartimaeus did three important things.

He Cried Out

We need to cry to the Lord for mercy, forgiveness, and salvation. In the Bible, it is described as repentance and faith. We should acknowledge that we are sinners and should turn from our sin. Just like with Bartimaeus, the Lord wants to hear from our own lips our need of forgiveness.

He Cast Off

We read how Bartimaeus cast away his cloak because it might hinder him and become an obstacle. So too there may be things in our lives—habits, friends, doubts—that are hindering us from coming to Christ. We must discard them.

He Came

And most important, as Bartimaeus came to Jesus, you need to come to Him. You may have all sorts of good thoughts about Jesus and who He is. You may even understand why He died on the cross. But you will receive your spiritual sight and salvation only if you come to Him.

By His Spirit, Jesus is calling today, "Come unto Me!" Jesus told His disciples, "The one who comes to Me I will by no means cast out" (John 6:37 NKJV).

The sad thing is that people do not want to come because they are blind to their need. Jesus said, "But you are not willing to come to Me that you may have life" (John 5:40 NKJV).

I mention another word beginning with the letter C, *compassion*. The Lord Jesus Christ's compassion motivated Him to go to the cross, and He is grieved today that some people do not want to open their minds and see what a wonderful salvation He has provided. I urge you to think about these things.

May the Lord bless His Word to all your hearts, and may you enjoy these meditations, which are intended to bring comfort and draw you closer to the Lord Jesus.

Bible quotations are from the King James Version unless indicated by the following abbreviations.

TLB: The Living Bible
NLT: New Living Translation
NIV: New International Version
ESV: English Standard Version
ASV: American Standard Version
NKJV: New King James Version
NASB: New American Standard Bible
NASU: New American Standard Updated
RSV: Revised Standard Version
AMP: Amplified New Testament

About the Author

David Purchase, B.A, FCA, is a retired accountant. He was born in 1936 in Cardiff on the South Wales coast. He lives there now in retirement with his wife Eva, having lived in Newcastle-under-Lyme in Staffordshire for thirty years. They have recently celebrated their Diamond Wedding anniversary. They have three children and six grandchildren. At a youth camp in 1948 he trusted the Lord Jesus as his Saviour. He has been a church elder for over fifty years and he has been involved with gospel work among people of all ages for over 70 years; with Sunday schools, Boys Brigade, church youth groups, young people's camps and Bible teaching week-end conferences, and lay preaching. For many years he visited many care homes for the elderly, with a team singing favourite hymns and giving gospel talks.

Printed in the United States
by Baker & Taylor Publisher Services